SAYING GOODBYE TO DAD

A Journey through Grief of Loss of a Parent

SAYING GOODBYE TO DAD

UNDERSTANDING THE MOURNING AND GRIEVING PROCESS OF LOSING A FATHER

MANDY WARCHOLA

Copyright © 2012 Mandy Warchola
All rights reserved.
ISBN: 1470048477
ISBN-13: 978-1470048471

Contents

PREFACE

Do not go gentle into that good night,
Old age should burn and rave at close of day;
Rage, rage against the dying of the light

Dylan Thomas

That was the last conversation I had with my father. If only I had known, I might have kept him on the phone longer, and said a few more words. Words of what, I don't know. I might have said words of encouragement, maybe of regret of things we had not done or said, maybe pleaded with him to wait for me to get there, or maybe I would have just kept him on the phone saying nothing just to keep the conscious connection with him going, knowing it would be our last conversation. What would one say, if one knew for sure it would be the last conversation you would ever have with your beloved parent? This was mine.

I could hear the far off telephone tone ringing 14,000 miles away. It rang twice and my mother's voice came on the line.
"Mom, it's me" I said apprehensively, hoping that anxiety wasn't showing itself on the other end of the line.

"Hello Mandy" my mother answered in a hushed voice.
"How is he doing?" I asked, lowering my tone as if I had to be quiet on this end of the phone, although no-one was around me.
"He's all right for now, he's settled into the hospital room, and has bandages on him where he fell this morning." She whispered.

"What happened, Mom?" I asked, trying to hold back the desperate anguish I felt.

"Well" she paused resignedly, and I could hear the sadness and despair in her voice, and then resumed "He got up in the middle of the night, saw my night light on, and walked around the bed to switch it off. While he was up, he slipped and fell, and couldn't get up. He cried out for help, and I had to get your brother to help get him off the floor. He was bleeding all over the place"

"Oh, no! What can I do?" The familiar dread sinking into my stomach.

"Nothing right now, do you want to speak to him?" She asked me.

"Yes, I'd love to. Is he okay to talk?" I asked.

"Yes, hold on." I hear her talking to my dad; "Siggy, Mandy's on the phone and wants to talk to you."

My dad's voice comes onto the line, and sounds so far off to me. "Hello my darling".

"Hello, dad!" I emphasize the 'Hello' just like I always do to show him only confidence, and not how I really feel about the possible dreaded prospect of losing him.

"How are you doing? I hear you've been in the wars."

"I'm doing great!" He replies weakly but at the same time, defiantly strong similar to what I've heard from him, my entire life. "I have your mother, brother and sister here, and I'm being looked after very nicely by the nurses."

"I'm glad to hear that, dad" I said, with tears brimming in my eyes.

"I'm still going to come to America and visit you, you know" he stated.

I laughed lightly in surprise at that.

"Don't laugh!" he said: "I mean it!"

I smiled through my tears "I know you do, dad. I'll let you get back to your visitors now. Take care of yourself."

"I will" he said.

"Bye dad" I said quietly.

"I love you!" he said. This surprised me, as it wasn't his normal style of ending a phone call.

"I love you too".

The phone went dead.

That night, my brother called, and told me the doctor had said that the rest of the family was to return from the United States immediately. It was 10:00 pm on Tuesday night, and I hurriedly booked a ticket, and arrived at the airport at 6:00 am, only to be informed my flight was cancelled.

At one of the worst times in my life, I was treated with complete contempt by United Airlines as I begged for help, telling them my father was dying, and I needed to get there quickly. A grey haired women who was supervising the passengers waiting, looked at me without expression, telling me to get back in line with everyone else. To no avail. I lay sobbing on the floor of United Airlines at Los Angeles International Airport in a line that was completely ignored for three hours, while watching others get onto the next flight. I kept calling the toll free number of the carrier, to no avail. There was to be no help for me in my predicament whatsoever. After 6 long anguished hours of standby, I finally got on a flight which had a layover of nine hours in Frankfurt.

I doubt I could ever explain in words, the frustration, anxiety, desperation and hopelessness I felt during all those wasted hours of waiting to get to my final destination. It's hard to remember how many times I went into the bathroom on the airplane and in the airports and sobbed. No matter what I did to try and speed things up, nothing worked.

Finally I arrived in South Africa, where my sister met me at the airport. I was excited to see her, and she was smiling, no doubt

pleased to see me too. As I started to hug her, I said, "Come on, let's get to the hospital!"
As I looked at her, I saw a single tear flow from one of her eyes, and she said "Mandy, he passed away yesterday..."

I remember crumbling in her arms sobbing loudly, not caring about all the people around me staring. All the torment, anguish and lamenting in vain. All the rushing, waiting in long lines impatiently, begging unsympathetic airline help, and pleading was for nothing. It was too late.

My darling father Siegfried Michelson, nicknamed Siggy, died at 3:40 pm on July 28th, 2011 at the ripe young age of 84, in a hospital bed. In the absence of his wife of almost sixty years, and with three of his five children and his sister by his side, he reluctantly conceded to death.

It had been just a year since he was diagnosed with Chronic Lymphatic Leukemia, and my father did not want to die, even though he had in fact stated many times that he was ready to die. I was told, that in the end, he flailed his arms and looked at his family in desperation, knowing that he was dying, and hoping someone could help him.

I had tried during my 3 visits during the preceding nine months to give him various self help remedies, including hypnosis, Qigong (Ancient Chinese healing pronounced Chi-gong), and teaching him to have positive thoughts and statements. Only on my last trip, when he was in the final stage of his illness, did he start trying some of the techniques, and temporarily felt better. Unfortunately, it was too late.

The whirl of the next few days, after I arrived from the airport, could have been something out of a Woody Allen movie. The busyness of scurrying around preparing for a funeral and adequate food, arguing who was going to sleep where, and who

Page | 14

was going to perform which function, was perplexing and frustrating to me. I moved through those days incognizant of my feelings, showing up when needed and mindlessly following other peoples instructions.

I remember this feeling of extreme numbness, almost as if I was disembodied from everything and everyone. To be honest, that feeling lasted well through the funeral. It was almost as if I was on auto-pilot. I realize now, that this was very much the normal way people deal with loss and death, by this feeling of numbness and disbelief, and keeping very busy so one doesn't have time to think, never mind actually feel. The feeling part comes later, when everything settles down, and everyone has gone their own ways, and all that is left is the quiet bewilderment and the contemplation of the loss.

When I returned to the United States, 10 days later, I started looking for ways to deal with my grief as my mother now seemed to be taken care of. What I noticed is that ***the world carries on oblivious to your loss.*** I found in my research that more information and books have been written for the widow's benefit, than the surviving adult child. I tried to go back to work, to be hit with pangs and waves of grief at unexpected moments.

This preface covers my own personal story of grief and bereavement, told from an adult perspective, of the loss of a father. The information I will give you in this book, will cover the various stages of grief and mourning, so you will know what to expect. I will also give you ideas of where to look for help outside of your own environment. *Where you see a paragraph and text in italics, those are my personal thoughts and feelings, throughout the journey of my loss.* There are many resources available, some of which I will write about. It's hard to have to search for help once you are already in the midst of painful grieving for a parent.

Whether you are expecting a future loss, or you have already experienced one, this information will hopefully prepare and inspire you, just as my research for the material of this book inspired me. At the end, there will be a list of recommended reading, from which you most definitely will find inspiration and understanding of the whole process. This is not just a personal story, but is also an accumulation of research from a non-technical, non-professional viewpoint.

I hope to provide you with a clear path or map of how to proceed through your grief like I did. The path does have a beginning, middle and an end, but it's the journey along the path, that will hopefully turn out to be worthwhile for you. Included along the way, will be some philosophies of life, death and beyond, which I believe in. You can take what you like and leave the rest. So let's begin.

1 THE EVENT

Life is real! Life is earnest!
And the grave is not its goal;
Dust thou art; to dust returnest,
Was not spoken of the soul.

- Henry Wadsworth Longfellow

I remember driving back from the airport, on the way back to my sister's house, where the funeral arrangements were in full swing. I sat in shock, numbness and misery, feeling helpless over what was transpiring. I realized I had no control over my father's death.

For me, it was chaos and confusion. Why didn't he wait for me? This was an event which has changed my life forever. At the funeral I was powerless, unable to see his body, prohibited by religious customs. The coffin was so small and plain, and I wondered how my dad's body could fit in there. Even though I am in shock, I feel like I'm screaming inside, and that no one can hear me. I tried so hard to get there in time, and now, all I have is this empty, lost feeling inside. How can I ever recover from this?

The fact that I had missed the most important event of being with my dad when he passed, and was now showing up in time to watch the frenetic funeral activities commence, had left me almost devoid of feeling. I did not want to be part of the funeral plans. I did not want to participate in the removal of my father from the living. I wanted to see my father's body, because I couldn't believe he was really dead. No one would let me see him. It was against "custom" they said. So I was to spend the rest of my life, believing his body was really squeezed into that tiny little coffin?

Everyone was so busy, running around, preparing food, acting in a businesslike manner. I was just so numb and in pain, that I couldn't even cry. I just sat there in misery, feeling disjointed from my body. No one took the time to sit and really talk to me to discover how I was really feeling. I suppose as everyone was dealing with their grief in their own way, I was unreasonable to expect that intense communication that I wanted.

My father was buried according to the orthodox Jewish tradition, a tradition that I did not agree with, as he had not lived his life in an orthodox way. Personally, it felt wrong to me for him to be buried in that manner (in a plain small coffin, with a sheet wrapped around him). I guess as he was such a larger than life, powerful man, I expected a powerful ending, not this sad quiet one. Reluctantly I had to participate. My anger was suppressed into depression. I don't remember much of that weekend, except helplessness and despair. The misery of sitting through three nights of prayers with people I didn't know commiserating the loss of someone who was so important to me, is hard to describe. After the first night, I had had enough. He was buried on a Sunday. The family sat in the front row. I turned behind me to see the people who had shown up, and didn't recognize anyone. This did not feel like reality and I wished I was anywhere else.

The larger the family, the very much more complicated things are. Many spend a large amount of time at the deathbed, waiting for the final moment of their loved ones lives. At the time of death, for the people who are actually there, there is a definite closure. You can't deny that someone has died when you actually see their last breath. The final exhalation catches you unaware, as you wait for the next breath in. After you've waited for about 30 seconds, it dawns on you that was their final breath. When you look at the body, all you see is a carcass of a human being. The essence is gone. It's important to see and know that. When you are not present, you have to accept the death from the words of others.

Many people want to be there for that final moment because of the importance and finality of the death event. There is something very spiritual about seeing a person take their last breath. It is a comforting feeling to some, rather than a horror, of course depending on the type of death. I have seen someone die, and it was peaceful, however, I didn't get to see my father's death. There are many times when people pass on, that loved ones have left for a break. The people who need to be there for those final moments are present.

My mother left my father's bedside in the hospital after being there constantly for two days, to go home and freshen up to come back to be back next to her husband. When she got back less than two hours from the time she had left, he had passed away. He had also passed away less than 24 hours before I got there. Many times I have wondered why my father didn't wait until I got there, or why he waited until my mother left. Could it be the two of us would have suffered more for seeing it? I wish I knew the answerI believe that the dying choose their moments carefully, according to who will best be able to handle the passing on of their soul. The ones who will be most affected, and most devastated, will not be present at the time of passing.

The Last Moments

If your parent has had a long illness, every last moment you are able to spend with them is precious. No matter how long we have lived, or how old we are, we are never quite prepared for that final moment of the death of our beloved parent. We want to be there with them, prevent their pain, post pone their death as long as possible, but ultimately our attempts to do that are futile. We end up helplessly watching the parent we so loved pass away. That curtain of death, which opens up at the instance of passing, gives us a brief moment where we get to understand the complexity of life. Then it closes again, leaving some of us with emptiness, loss and confusion, and others with hope and relief.

The cause of the death

Depending on the cause of the death of your beloved parent, the reactions vary due to a number of factors. One of the main factors is how your parent died. If the death was sudden, as a result of a car accident, the shock of the loss is instant and overwhelming. If the death was long and drawn out, such as the result of a terminal illness, although the sadness is great, it is expected and anticipated, and can be accompanied with a reluctant form of relief at the passing. Being present at your parent's death is important to almost everyone. From them you were created and the intense bond that formed from your birth to their death can never be broken.

Often people report that the death occurred when they had left for the night, gone home to take a shower, or even just left the room at the hospital to go to the bathroom. After that, guilt descends upon people, who then spend much time agonizing over things such as "I wish I had stayed longer" or "I wish someone would have called me to let me know the death was imminent" or (in my case) "Why couldn't he have waited just one more day for me to get there?" . I personally have only seen one person pass on, and it was very peaceful, not at all like my father's passing was explained to me. Not seeing the actual death can leave one with an experience of unresolved loss without closure.

We all know that one day, we are going to die, but somehow it seems to be something that's very far off into the future. The feelings of devastation and loss are so immense that our immune system kicks in an automatic protection factor called shock. When someone close to us dies, the very first thing that we experience is this shock.

The initial shock of the loss

One of the very first feelings experienced when being told of a death of a loved one, is immediate flood of feelings, an intense emotional reaction. There might be a complete breakdown on the spot, an immense surge of uncontrolled grief in the form of tears. Afterwards, when the tears subside, as with shock, there are generally feelings of disorientation and bewilderment.

One might experience being in an anesthetized state of numbness . This is the body's defense mechanism kicking in, to prevent possible hurt. You would go into an immobilized kind of daze. Similar to the fight or flight syndrome of anxiety which dates back to the old caveman days of being in constant fear for one's life, so that one would either 'fight' or 'take flight'(flee a situation).

In my case, it wasn't a shock of a sudden unexpected death. My father had cancer and I knew he was going to die in the not too distant future, I just didn't know when. That doesn't make the loss any less, but different than that of a sudden unexpected death such as a fatal heart attack or car accident.

Reactions at the time of death

The initial reactions to the death of one's parent may vary but only for the first stage of shock. Once the shock starts to subside, the mourning is pretty much consistent, depending on the closeness of the family relationships with the deceased.

If the loss is sudden, such as an accidental violent death, suicide or heart attack, or expected, such as after a long illness, the initial phases of grief can be different.

Sudden loss of a parent

With sudden loss, one is unable to adequately say goodbye, and there may be unfinished business which can lead to guilt and regret further down the road. If the death was violent, then there will be the added emotion of anger towards the perpetrator combined with shock and grieving. Our bodies could experience the loss on a physiological level differently. Many factors influence shock and grief of a sudden loss, and questions arise to the extent of the following:

- Could this have been prevented?
- Might this have had a different result had our parent been in different care?
- Was there anything in particular you could have done to change or prevent the outcome?
- If it was suicide, would it have helped to listen or observe more?
- If it was a car accident, was the mechanic who did the last checkup to blame?
- Did you let them know you loved them the last time you saw them, or did you say goodbye angrily?

All these questions can come up, and really for the most part, they aren't relevant, even though you feel they are. Anger and grief over the passing can affect how we view insignificant things, and cause us to unnecessarily place blame on anyone and anything. *It's important to remember, as time passes, these feelings of intense anger and wanting to blame an extraneous source will subside.*

Expected loss of a parent

When your parent has died from a long illness, and it was an inevitable event, there can be many different feelings, ranging from mourning, guilt and even relief. I've heard people discuss the death of a parent, stating they were glad their parent had passed and the suffering was over. At the same time, that individual felt extreme guilt over feeling relief over the passing of their parent. There are no wrong and right ways to feel. Everybody experiences the loss of a parent in their own way, with many commonalities to the grief. Go easy on yourself, and realize that it's okay to feel whatever you are feeling, as long as it's not destructive in any way to yourself. If it is, then you need to consider professional help to get you through this particularly hard grieving period.

When your parent dies, the relationship still exists on a spiritual level, but it's very difficult to realize this in the beginning stages of mourning. The initial trauma and confusion of losing the person who gave you advice, who comforted you when you were low, and who was always unconditionally there for you, become apparent when the shock subsides, and reality sets in. It's alarming to know that you no longer have that support system in place, and you have now become the adult.

If you were the caretaker of your father, and you agonizingly hung in over the last final months of his illness, there might be guilty feelings of relief. It's this feeling of relief which might actually torment you which will really puts stress on your body. Even in these early stages of grief, it's important to acknowledge that there was nothing else you could have done to prevent the passing.

2 THE FIRST FEW DAYS

You're not fully an adult until you've lost a parent

Fay Schmidt

Being the youngest of five children, and the baby of the family, I was particularly close to my parents. As a child, I was allowed to climb into their bed, between them, where I would happily fall asleep, until sent to bed. Even as an adult, when I visited my parents, I used to climb into their bed, in between both of them, just for fun, and relish the memories of the feeling of safeness and security. The week after my father had passed, knowing my mother was feeling that loss, I would get into bed next to her until she fell asleep. After almost sixty years of sleeping next to the same person every night, one of the hardest things for her is to get used to that empty spot. Losing my father felt like I had lost a body part which I could never get back. I could only imagine, my mother felt much, much worse.

Almost exactly a year before my father died, he was diagnosed with Chronic Lymphatic Leukemia, which can indicate a lengthy slow decline. I started grieving the same way a year before his death as I did after his death. The feeling was no less intense. I knew I was going to lose him. Panic and dread filled me and I felt helpless but also determined to help him whichever way I could. I did what I could to encourage him to heal, to give him strength. I didn't want my father to see how scared I was. I started travelling to see him and supplied him with self-hypnosis CD's and books *on self healing. By the time he died, I was filled with regret that I hadn't tried harder. I finally had to acknowledge and accept that I had no control over his living or dying. I had been in deep anguish over the inevitability of his death.*

Accepting the reality of death

We all live in fear of death. It's difficult for us to accept the fact that we are going to die. None of us are prepared to die. When it happens, even though we have put it off as something that won't happen to us, the very nature of the termination of our human experience is terrifying to us. We pretend it's not going to happen to us, even though we start noticing our friends being afflicted with it. We're raised with an intense fear of death, rather than with a calming spiritual approach of death being a part of life, and the next adventure which is waiting for us. We're taught death is something to fear, as opposed to something to welcome.

No matter what our spiritual beliefs, it doesn't take away the sense of loss, or the anguish of losing a loved one. There is always a part of us, however spiritual we are, that doubts the existence of anything after death. So when we see our beloved parent, in a coffin at their funeral, there is something very final, which confirms the reality of the death in our minds.

I needed the closure of seeing my father's body, and I was not allowed to have it. This left me with a sense of powerless, helplessness and anger. I have anger issues against my family for not allowing me to have that closure, although in retrospect, it wasn't anyone's deliberate intention to deny me that closure. The anger has subsided as I realized this was also part of my grief and anger at myself for not making it in time for his death.

What to expect right after the funeral

At and directly after the funeral, there is a sense of bewilderment, disorientation and disbelief. You could feel as if you're walking into a movie of someone else's drama. It takes a while to fully comprehend the loss. Even as you watch your parent being buried, it's almost as if you're partaking in a dream rather than reality. This is all the initial shock. You will find people will walk up to you saying random types of statements such as "He had a long life" or "Sorry for your loss" or "At least he isn't suffering", as well as many other strange, well-meaning comments. Inside you will feel like screaming, but to the outside world, you will appear morose and helpless as an unwilling participant in a sad play.

Right after the funeral, when the flurry of people has died down, and all that's left behind is the immediate family, the sense of loss becomes more profound. When you lose your father, the stability of the family becomes extremely fragile, and this is a particularly vulnerable time for the widow. This is a time when the griever may make hasty decisions without using discerning judgment. It's preferable to just concentrate on mourning for those first few days, and not make any major life-altering decisions.

In my family, the second day after my father's funeral, my mother was encouraged to buy a new car, put her house up for sale, and put an offer in to buy an extremely expensive place for her to move to. I was unable to sit back and watch this without questioning it. When I was told that an offer to purchase this extremely expensive property was being made two days after the funeral, I objected as I believed this was not a clearly thought out decision. At the same time this was going on, my father's clothing and possessions were rapidly being cleared out, so as almost to flush his presence from the house. In a family meeting that day, the day after my father's funeral, I told the whole family they were rushing through decisions that would affect my mother's future. I insisted that this transition was much too quick, and needed to be better thought out. As a result, there was a breakdown in the relationships between myself and the rest of my family.In retrospect, I could have been more diplomatic, as emotions were high. That was the day my family fell apart. I realized without my dad around, we were no longer a functional unit, and that it was my dad that had kept us together. Five days later I returned to the USA to mourn the death of my father on my own. Undoubtedly, this was one of the most difficult times of my life.

Since this event, my mother felt everything was moving too quickly, and even though she put her house up for sale, the sale never went through. She then decided to stay there, in the meantime, because the house reminded her of my dad, and how happy they were there together. So everything happened as it was meant to. Almost a year after my father's passing, my mother sold her home and moved to be closer to the rest of the family.

Family Relationships in play

As you can tell from what happened to me, family relationships become extremely strained after the death of one's parent. This is the time when financial discussions happen about the surviving parent, and about how financial matters are to be handled. This is also when inheritance issues are dealt with. It's at this time that the troublesome part of family dynamics may surface, particularly in larger families where the interactions of sibling rivalry are in play. I heard someone say, that the only family without dysfunction are families of one. Keeping that in mind, beware of the dysfunctions of a family getting in the way of good common sense. Take your time, and think through events concerning the future. Don't keep quiet if you think ill-advised decisions are being made. If you are a part of the family you deserve to have a part of the decision making, or at the very least, to have your opinion heard. Stand up for what you believe is right. I don't regret what I said that day although I could have worded things a little more diplomatically, but the intent was absolutely correct. Even in my grief, I intuitively knew that mourning makes people do irrational things. There's a difference between being right and being hurtful. Try to get your rationalization across in a manner that isn't hurtful or accusatory.

Reactions to Shock

There can usually be several aspects that contribute to shock after the loss of one's parent. Below are two of the ways we react to shock which are general physical symptoms and general emotional symptoms, whether the loss was unexpected or expected.

General Physical Symptoms of Emotional Shock

When a death of a parent occurs, nothing prepares you for how you will initially feel. You may think that shock is just an immediate reaction, but in actuality it can last for quite a while after the loss. In fact, quite some time can go by, and you may feel you are back to normal, only to re-experience the symptoms of shock. Here are some physical symptoms experienced from shock:

- Walking around in a numbed daze.
- Feeling spacey and disoriented.
- Drops or changes in blood pressure,
- Dizziness, nausea.
- Lack of energy, and lethargy.
- Difficulty with decision making.

- Anxiety, with possible feelings of claustrophobia
- Inability to react with emotion, even though intellectually you know there is something you should be experiencing.

General Mental Symptoms of Emotional Shock

The emotional part of shock is just as disturbing and unexpected as the physical symptoms, especially as it has never been experienced in this context prior to the loss. The first time you experience the death of someone close to you, you have nothing to compare the experience to. You've seen others lose family members, and comforted others, but never experienced the actual feeling of loss of a parent. You may have contemplated the experience in dread, but the first time it happens, it's different from what you expected. Expect this difference, and recognize it. It will help you get through what is yet to come.

The symptoms of emotional shock mentioned below are some of what you can expect.

- Isolation or withdrawing from social interactions or communications with others. Not wanting to be the center of attention.
- Preferring to be by oneself.
- Forgetfulness such as wondering why one walked into a room, or sudden loss of thought or confusion in the middle of a sentence.
- Inability to interact with others.
- Inability and unwillingness to perform daily tasks which involve seeing others in their "normal" lives, at places such as the post office or supermarket.
- Not wanting to be anywhere where people look happy and unconcerned with your particular predicament.
- Not wanting to see the rest of the world turning while yours has stopped.

- Impulsive reactions to mundane ordinary events.
- Jumping the gun - Reaction instead of Action. Instead of taking time to consider the ramifications of an action, one might react in a way outside of the ordinary.

How everyone reacts differently to shock of a death

Each person can take the news of the death differently. During the shock phase, right at the beginning, the true impact of the loss is not yet experienced. You might think people are handling the death relatively well, as they are not being emotional but in reality, this is just the phase of shock. When time passes, and the shock phase seems to be over, you will notice true reactions to the loss.

The following describes just some of the different reactions experienced due to the intense emotional shock of losing one's father. The main intent here is to make known to you the fact that what you are experiencing is really normal, even though it doesn't feel like it. Every human being on the planet will experience your loss sooner or later, and will feel what you feel. You are not alone.

- Some people immediately react, and others might suppress a reaction until a later time, while walking around in a daze, trying to process what has happened.
- The closeness of the relationship to the deceased can also be a contributing factor to how the news is reacted to. This has similarities to the fact that it might take a different individuals different amount to time to recover from grieving or mourning of a loss.
- The core beliefs and spiritual acceptances of living and dying, widely varies from individual to individual, and can also make a difference to people's reactions.

- Some people may be unconsciously agitated, not wanting to deal with emotions, and keeping busy by watching TV, constantly talking and wanting company so as not to be alone.

When losing one's father, one has lost the most stable force in one's life. Our father was there when we were born, and was the rock that stood by and protected us while we grew into adults. This person was a constant in our lives, that was never questioned. The thought that our parent may not be there one day, was so terrifying that we sent that thought to the back of our minds, where hopefully it would not bug us. Without our parent's protection, we would not have survived as infants. Even though we reached adulthood and moved on with our adult lives, we still always felt we had that fatherly love and support available at any time we needed it. Then, as an adult, the loss of that comforting protection completely shakes the foundation of our world, even though we function perfectly well without our fathers being in our lives. We marry, we have our own children and lives, but that never takes away the original stability and steadfastness we received from our dads.

It is said that being with someone at the time of death opens the curtain to all those still living, of the world of the unknown. This allows you to see into the world of death, just for a brief moment, and then the curtain closes again. That's why so many hospital staff and family members present at the time of a death, have reported seeing the dying person talking to dead relatives in the room. It's speculated at the time of death that the dying see their loved ones and friends who have come to help them make the transition. Recently, the sister of deceased Apple executive Steve Job wrote an article where she revealed that her brother's final words were "Wow, Oh Wow!", while he looked into the air past the family. One can only speculate the welcoming wondrous things he saw at his moment of death.

Shock and other causes of Disorganization

Initial shock, which can last for several weeks, is a period of disorganization. This will include feelings of almost out of control disarray and forgetfulness. This could comprise of finding oneself somewhere without remembering how we got there, and inability of being able to get things done. Shock and disorganization almost take precedence over actual grieving at this stage.

When accident victims experience trauma, they are actually not in pain directly after the accident. It's almost as if an inbuilt pain protection factor kicks in. A friend once told me he was in a bad motorcycle accident and went head first into a car. When the paramedics arrived on the scene, he said he felt perfectly fine, as they looked at him in horror. His face had completely caved in, and he could not feel anything due to the trauma.

Just like in this example, after the death of one's father, even if the passing was expected, the initial few weeks consist of shock and confusion. It can feel almost as if some of the pain is shut off by a automatic body protective function. The loss suspends us into a state of existing in an unreal impalpable environment. As some time goes by, severe disorientation and disorganization is consistently experienced. There is forgetfulness, and people often relate to walking into a room, and forgetting why they walked in their in the first place. This experience of just existing in a long lasting state of numbness is very normal. This state of confusion and disorganization can last several months and can overlap with the grief and mourning process. One is not mutually exclusive of the other.

As time goes by, you might look back at this period and completely have forgotten certain events that took place soon after the passing of your parent. During this period, the hopes one might have had of preventing this cataclysmic event slowly begin to dissipate, and a feeling of powerless might set in, as onc beings to acknowledge the reality of the loss.

When the Numbness wears off

When the initial numbness and shock start wearing off, this is when the full impact of the loss hits us. At this stage, when the reality of the situation sinks in, that we will never see our parent again, this is when full brunt of the pain hits us like a sledgehammer, and the tears start. This could begin a phase of real grief and depression. It's at this stage that it becomes critical to take care of ourselves, and our personal needs.

3 THE GRIEVING PROCESS

It feels like something you will never get over, but you do.

Carmen

Losing my father was one of the hardest experiences of my life. I remember returning to the United States, to find my house full of cheerful people. My brother-in-law, unbeknownst to me, had invited his son, daughter-in-law, and 3 kids (2 of which were very young) to stay in our house while we were gone. I returned grief stricken, eight days after my father had passed, to a large amount of people staying in our small house. All I could do was lock myself in my bedroom and only come out for meals, for about five days, until the house was empty again. I did not want to socialize or talk to anyone, so I kept to myself.

That week, I walked into the office, and looked around at everyone laughing and feeling happy, and felt like an alien. I was in a very painful place. To see others experiencing happiness, while I've had such a tremendous loss, was incomprehensible to me. I walked into the office of the person, whose team I was on, and he said. "Gee, I'm sorry for your loss", and then said "Come on, let's make some money!". I literally had to immediately leave and go home where I spent the next month, mourning on my own.

Differences between Grieving and Mourning

Grieving is the emotion that follows a loss, while mourning is the event of experiencing and processing the grief. The bereavement period is the period of time you spend mourning the loss of your loved one. These two emotions which are different are also very similar and do overlap onto one another. The meaning of bereavement is to be deprived by the death of someone who was valuable to you. The bereavement process is the process through this state of grief and mourning.

On Grief

Grief from mourning is the most undervalued of the human emotions in our society today. Even though loss of a parent, and the mourning thereof, is the one thing that unites us, due to the fact we are all going to go through it someday, it seems to be the one emotion no one wants to acknowledge. There are no exceptions to this in any of our lives as we will all lose someone we love at some stage. Whether it's a parent, a spouse, a sibling, or a precious friend, we are all going to experience loss. Some people turn away from the bereaved during the mourning process for a number of reasons, perhaps fear, or not wanting to be emotionally involved in the pain of another, or perhaps because of the anticipation of the loss of their own parent.

What is it about losing one's father that rings so deep in all of us? Our father being there at the beginning of our lives, and unconditionally loving us, even at times we felt unlovable, was one of the most stable consistent parts of our existence. It is difficult for us to imagine our lives sans our parent. Just the comfort of being able to pick up the phone and know we could chat, even if we lived quite a distance away.

When I see people who give very little empathy to others, I know that it's only a matter of time before they experience their own grief and loss. How do I know this? I was that person! I was the person who didn't know what to say to others who had suffered losses, who preferred not to go to funerals or stick around others who were sad. I had never been through a loss of my own. When my father died, for the first time I experienced the monumental impact of intense grief from the loss of a loved one. I had no idea of how the grief would make me feel, or of the magnitude of the loss, until it happened to me.

Someone experiencing bereavement for the first time is completely devastated by the array of emotions experienced, from anger to denial, to withdrawal and guilt. You need people to spend time with you and just let you talk. Someone needs to be there for you while you experience the worst sadness and pain of your life.
Shock, numbness and disbelief will fade leaving behind deep sadness, grief and mourning, as one faces the enormity of the loss.

Many of us fear that facing this enormous loss will be too much for us, and that the intense emotional grief will somehow overwhelm us. If the grief is acknowledged, it will eventually dissipate. Grief that is unacknowledged keeps reappearing.

Most western societies expect someone to get over the loss, let's say in a month, although in reality, after two weeks people stop inquiring after the bereaved. Work environments give people three days to mourn, and then they are expected to come back to work and function normally. Only someone who has gone through this process truly understands that grieving will not be complete within the short timeframes that are given to us by society.

The purpose of mourning

There is a purpose to mourning, even though it does not feel like it. It may feel like an eternity of sadness is ahead of you, but really it isn't. The purpose of mourning is not only to pay tribute to our parent who has passed, but also to allow ourselves time to heal.

A friend of mine made the quote at the beginning of the chapter to me, before my father had passed, while I was discussing the gloomy outlook with her, based on the experience of the loss of her own parents. " *It feels like something you will never get over, but you do.*" I didn't really understand what she meant by that, because I couldn't comprehend the full impact of grief at that time. I understand now. It does feel like the grief is never ending. When you're happy time flies by, but when you're sad, it crawls by. Nonetheless, with either emotion, time does go by. So, as the old saying goes, *this too shall pass.* Know that there is an end to how bad you will feel, and that in time, you will feel a gradual shedding of the sadness.

When I returned to my home, I found that none of my friends were contacting me. I couldn't understand it. Where were my flowers? Where were sympathy cards? I realized then that it is very difficult, even for your close friends to deal with your mourning over the loss of a parent. This also holds true to close acquaintances whom you frequently associate with. I actually had to call up friends to ask them to meet me for coffee. I felt so isolated and lonely during that time. Once my friends saw I was okay to hang out with, and that I didn't break down constantly, they started coming back into my life with full force. Now I have to make excuses not to go out all the time. It is said, the true number of friends one has can be counted on one hand. I can verify that.

During that first month, I slept in every day, found a bereavement counselor and group to go to. I researched the process of grief and mourning and what the effects were, as well as purchased books on bereavement. I had to understand what I was going through, because it was nothing like anything I had ever experienced before. Nothing in my life prepared me for the experience of grief of losing my father.

What Grief Feels Like

During the first month, the grief over the loss of a parent is so intense, and baffling, that you feel out of control of any aspect of your life. Amidst much confusion, bewilderment and angst, realize that you're still going through the shock portion of your journey. Grief depletes us of energy and is overwhelming in its very nature.

"All events are blessings given to us to learn from."

Elisabeth Kübler-Ross

The stages of loss

I would like to acknowledge Elizabeth Kubler Ross's five stages of loss: Denial, Anger, Bargaining, Depression and Acceptance. I would also like to state that these were written specifically for people who were approaching death, to help them cope with their upcoming demise. Briefly to explain these would be the following breakdowns:

- Denial: "This isn't happening. I must be dreaming. It's not real. I'm not dying. It's a mistake."
- Anger: "This is not fair. Who's responsible? I need someone to blame. I'm angry at the world, at God, at everyone who I perceived to have landed this misfortune on me."
- Bargaining: "Please God, if you let me live, I will dedicate the rest of my life to you! I'll do anything, I'll work with the poor, I'll help feed starving children in Africa..etc."
- Depression: "I feel sad and realize that my life is over and I'm going to die."
- Acceptance: "I am not sad anymore. I realize that this is a part of life, and I accept it, and am ready to move on."

The above stages were catering to people who were dying. It's accepted that these stages are not specifically in the above order, but that's the general order of them. Once can bounce around back and forth between the different stages. These stages are now commonly used for defining the recovery from a loss of a loved one as well.

The stages discussed below were what I experienced, and noticed others experiencing, who were in the same position as myself. What I noticed was a very definite progression of emotions, similar to the original stages above, but different. For me, it didn't seem to fit into the neat package of the stages above.

Stages of loss from my perspective

- Shock: The actual reality that the parent has deceased. There is a feeling of being part of a dream that is not really happening. In this phase, there are actually fewer tears and just a general feeling of complete numbness and disorientation. Shock is accompanied by a strange spacey feeling, almost like being high from a particular type of drug. It is similar to a dissociative feeling which is accompanied by a lack of mental clarity, focus and cognition. Some might compare it to an out of body experience. Once the shock starts to subside, only then do we realize the full impact of the loss.

- Disbelief: At the time one receives the news of the loss of our beloved parent, whether we had been expecting it or not, it is unbelievable to us. There is a disbelief that our parent has died, and we need absolute confirmation of the fact. This can be whether one is actually present at the time of passing or not. Some need to actually see the body for confirmation of the death, and others may just be convinced by the expression of the news bearer.

- Intense Grief/Depression/Weeping: After disbelief and shock wears off, the true impact and the finality of the event hits us, and then the intense pain of the loss is felt. At this stage we experience seemingly neverending uncontrollable misery and crying over our loss. The full impact of never being able to see our parent again has now resounded to our core, and we go through severe suffering and anguish. This is the time we need to be able to mourn and cry as much as we want, without restrictions of behavior put onto us by others. We need to be able to talk to others and be comforted about the loss, and be consoled, all at our own pace. There is no rushing through the grief. Depression is commonly associated with grief. This is an extremely important time to look after one's physical health. During this period, our sleep and appetite may be affected. Loss of appetite and insomnia, which are common symptoms of depression, are also strongly correlated with bereavement.

- Slight Improvement: As the weeks go by, the gaps between the crying bouts start becoming longer. Hardly noticeable, as time passes, other interests start working their way into our consciousness. Thought of getting together with friends, or going for walks, or getting back to work will slightly deviate our thoughts away from our loss, and will become more dominant as time passes.
- Intense Grief for a shorter period of time accompanied by Depression and Weeping: The grief returns at unexpected moments, and feels as intense as right at the beginning of the loss. Triggers such as a song in the supermarket, or a familiar item, can bring back the immense feelings of loss at any time.
- Slight Improvement: Even longer periods of time between weeping.
- The phases of intense grief and slight improvement continue swapping for quite a while, with the grief lessening. These slight improvements becoming more frequent and noticeable.
- Accepting the loss, becoming more content and part of society again. Feeling of renewed energy and joy. Going out with friends, seeing movies, working, enjoying life again and laughing.

- Relapses into grief, less frequently. There are still moments of sadness and reflection and occasional tears when alone.
- Acceptance of the loss. The loss is now a reality, and part of one's existence. The departed parent is never forgotten, but the loss is accepted and realized.
- Reminders of the loss over holidays. Holidays that were spent honoring our parent, like Father's Day, Thanksgiving, Christmas, can re-activate the grief. This will pass, and as the years go by, become an acceptable, expected sadness on that day.

The difference between Grief and Mourning

Grief is the feeling that accompanies many types of losses. Not necessarily death, but many other major events of one's life can cause grief such as divorce, separation, loss of a job, and many other unfortunate expected or unexpected situations. The grief varies according to the intensity of the relationship of the loss of a loved one.

Mourning is the way that grief is expressed, and is most common after the passing of a loved one. Bereavement is the grief period that follows the death. A parent's love was there since the beginning of your life. After death, the love felt does not die, but carries on, even though that parent no longer physically exists.

Many religions have different mourning traditions and periods that people might follow. Mourning is the outward expression of sorrow at someone's death. It encompasses a time period that someone is expected to show the public that they are in a period of grieving. Grieving and mourning are both necessary and expected to enable someone to get through the chaos of death, and start living their own life again. Grieving is completely normal after a loss. It's helpful to know that what you are going through is not completely unique and that others have experienced it too. For a while, you may wonder how you will cope with the intense feelings of sadness, and this is why literature on grieving and mourning is important.

I was so unprepared for the onslaught of emotions that I felt, when my grief first started, that I thought there might be something physically wrong with me. I did not understand the overwhelming physical and emotional effects that grief would have on my body.

The Physical Symptoms of Grief:

When you are past the initial shock and disbelief stage, as you head into the uncharted territories of full blown mourning, you might start to experience physical symptoms. These symptoms could be much like the symptoms experienced during depression or experienced by a lesser loss such as a breakup, divorce or loss of employment.

However, you might be so distracted by the overwhelming feelings you are experiencing, that you overlook what is physically happening to you. Grief can take a huge toll on our bodies. Some of the physical symptoms of grief might be so subtle. that time may pass before you even realize that you have these symptoms. If unattended, the physical symptoms, caused by emotional distress, could turn into something severe where medical attention is needed. Here are some of the physical symptoms you might experience. This will help in understanding that the symptoms you are experiencing are directly correlated to the loss of your loved one. This will give you the ability to try to help your body deal with the onslaught of these physical symptoms caused by grief, and to understand how they are all interconnected.

1. Stress: It's well known that chronic stress can be the cause of many physical issues and create havoc in your body. Stress can cause physical reactions right throughout your body, whether it be anxiety with panic attacks all the way to joint pain. It's important to find an effective way to handle your stress.

2. Stomach ache and digestive problems: These are some of the most common physical symptoms induced by stress. These can include a feeling of great pain in the upper part of the stomach, diarrhea or constipation as well as sudden urges to go to the bathroom, inability to control one's bowels. This could be similar to irritable bowel syndrome.

3. Nausea: Nausea is caused by physical symptoms such as too much stomach acid, or from a signal from the brain. In the case of grieving, all the messages are coming in from the brain, as the mind starts to comprehend the loss.

4. Headaches: Tension headaches are a common symptom of stress. Migraines, which are a more severe form of headache can cause great discomfort such as throbbing pain, sensitivity to light, nausea, and general discomfort.

5. Feeling tired all the time: A feeling of weakness, lethargy and tiredness is very common during the mourning period. This is also accompanied by a lack of energy and joy. There is little motivation to do anything such as exercising or having social contact with others.

6. Pains in chest: When people talk about being heartbroken from the death of a loved one, it can literally be a true statement, and manifest itself in heart issues. Intense feelings of anger can also cause chest pains. Stress can cause physiological responses, which in turn feeds into your circulation. Grieving sets off the "flight or fight"

stress response which can cause your blood pressure and heart rate to rise, this in turn places pressure on the heart. This causes your blood pressure and heart rate to increase, thereby placing more stress on your heart. This can damage the heart muscles, and/or could create an abnormal heartbeat amidst other even more serious problems.

7. Crying which seems uncontrollable.

8. Difficulty falling asleep or staying asleep.

9. Appetite disorders: Loss of interest in food, or indulging in excess food are very typical symptoms. Many people react differently to food, depending on how their previous behaviors regarding food were. Someone who stops eating when depressed, as opposed to someone who overeats, will continue those habits through the grieving period.

10. Breakdown in the immune system: Pre-existing arthritis could become noticeably worse. People have reported constantly having flu-like symptoms, or losing their voices.

11. Loss or gain of weight: This goes along with the appetite disorders. It's not something to be alarmed about unless the weight gain or loss is not slowing down, then medical attention might be needed.

12. Loss of sexual desire: It's well know that emotional problems are the biggest cause of sexual dysfunctions. A death would qualify as an emotional problem. Once someone has passed through the mourning period and starts to resume normal activities, sexual desire should go back to what it was before the loss.

The Emotional Symptoms of Grief:

I saw a family member go through a loss of a relationship. I asked if they had taken any medication, to deal with the loss, and they responded that they had not, as they knew it was a transitional grief where the intense feelings of sadness would subside after a period of time, and they would eventually return to normal.

This is true for most, as regards to the emotional symptoms of the loss of a parent. It is a good idea to seek medical support if the loss is overwhelming and the symptoms are not subsiding.

1. Depression: Most losses are accompanied by grief. If the grief does not reduce, but stays consistent, it can turn into depression. There are long-term and short-term depressions. Many of the depression symptoms are very similar to grieving symptoms.

2. Suicidal thoughts: A death makes one revalue one's own life. Many times, the ones left behind may go through a period where their own life no longer seems important without their loved one. Suicidal thoughts which occasionally appear should be taken note of. If these thoughts persist, a medical evaluation may be necessary.

3. Emotional Isolation: Wanting to stay away from others. Not wanting to be part of society because of the inability to relate to the world without one's parent in it.

4. Yearning and longing for the deceased parent: A feeling of abandonment by the parent who is deceased. Wishing that parent would somehow return to us and make us feel okay again.

5. Worrying and Guilt: This includes worrying about finances, or the remaining parent, or whether to go back to work, amidst many other personal concerns. Ruminating over what could have been, had something different before the parent's death been done. Guilt over events that could have been changed, had we done or not done a certain activity.

6. Absentmindedness, and forgetfulness: This includes misplacing things, forgetting important events. Not remembering why one walked into a room.

7. Fear: Now that one's parent has passed, one might feel next in line, and the fear of this horrendous event one day happening to us becomes a concern. Loss of one's parent brings the fears of our own mortality to the spotlight. We start wondering if the illness that caused our parent's death, could cause ours too.

8. Unwillingness to deal with the loss, which is the same as stifling feelings. This only prolongs the mourning period, as these feelings will resurface at a later stage.

9. Loneliness: Grieving for the loss of a parent is a lonely process. Only people who have the same type of relationship as you with your parent, or are experiencing a similar loss of their own, truly understand what you are going through. If you live far from your deceased parent and family, it's a very lonely time. Others around you are sympathetic, but they really don't understand or fully relate to your feelings of loss.

10. Anger; A common reaction to intense sadness and depression is anger. There is a propensity to blame someone or something for the intense agonizing pain which is being experienced. Anger towards family

members, including the deceased is common. Anger towards the doctors, for what they might or might not have done, is also not unusual.

Many people wonder if there was anything else they could have done to have helped the parent before they passed. There are often intense feelings of regret and guilt as obsessive thoughts of what might have been, are speculated over and over.

I wished I could have got to my father's bedside before he died. I also wished I had forced him to start trying different alternative healing strategies, and felt guilty that perhaps I didn't try hard enough. I could have been more insistent, and determined to help him get better from cancer. I could have take him to the east where many alternative medicines cure people. All these things plague me, as I helplessly acknowledge that what happened was inevitable, as well as pre-destined. I regret not going for walks with him, when he asked me to. Never did I realize that, when he's no longer around, I would agonize to do even these small things with him, that I thought never mattered, but they really do. I regret hurrying through conversations with him, because now, every word of his matters.

Grief eventually does diminish, if it is fully dealt with. The more knowledge and understanding we have about the grief process, the better we will be able to understand, process and move forward through the mourning process.

Expectations by Society

It's expected that those left behind will mourn. What is not expected or anticipated is the length of time someone will take to mourn the death of another. Society gives us about two weeks, and then we are expected to move on and participate in life's activities once more. Only someone who has actually been through a major loss, like the loss of one's father, can truly understand that the recovery period is not in absolutes, or black and white.

In conclusion, Grief is like a wound that needs to heal. The loss of a loved one is like a deep wound that has to have time to heal. You will always see the scar, and never forget the wound, but the pain will eventually go away.

4 ONE MONTH LATER

Nothing stays the same. Everything changes all the time

Mandy Warchola

After one month of losing my father, my life is chaotic. I am depressed, confused, distracted, and unable to function. I am angry and feel abandoned to have to find solace and comfort with strangers. How is it possible that with all the family I have, I am all alone, mourning my father in solitude. The loneliness is unbearable, and I find very little satisfaction in anything I do.

This is truly the worst event of my life. Who knew it would be this hard to lose one's father? It seems that even if you have a family of your own, the grief is no less devastating, confusing or intolerable. I wake up with gut wrenching pain in my stomach, unable to sleep, and unable to get up in the morning. I haven't been able to work, and find any type of pressure of society intolerable.

Although it is fully expected during our lives that one day we will lose our parent, when the moment actually arrives it's unlike anything you have prepared yourself for. The pain and confusion of the loss is devastating. The different reactions you go through are nothing like how you had envisioned yourself handling one of the most tragic events of your life. It makes no difference of how old your father was, or whether it was time for him to die, the grief you experience will still affect you to the core in a very primal way.

During the first month of losing one's father, the overwhelming feelings of grief need to be understood. Understanding the symptoms enables you to have some hope for the future, knowing that what you are experiencing has been experienced by others. There are others who are going through the same experiences as you, some simultaneously. There will be yet more who are still to experience the tragedy of loss of a parent.

For the First Month

For the first month, if you're lucky enough to have someone else as the breadwinner, or can afford to take time off from work, take the necessary time off to regroup. It's extremely difficult to concentrate and be functional, so allow yourself time to grieve and nurture yourself. Be kind and gentle with yourself, the same way you would treat someone you love who was ill. Work through bereavement as if it's an illness, for which you need time and care to recover.

This is the time to seek out support groups, or professional help from a bereavement counselor. Talk to your close friends and go for coffee. Stay away from hectic events if you can, because there you will see happy people again. In those situations, it's best to just not go, because firstly, you don't want to be a downer to others, and secondly, you might have to explain to people why you are sad, which will stir up your emotions, and make them uncomfortable. This is just until you can talk about the passing without feeling intensely emotional. It takes time to work through this. There is no shortcut around grief. It's a one step in front of the other process. It's not like a book, where you can skip past the pages you don't like. It's your life and you need to turn a page at a time, and acknowledge what's written on that page before you move to the next one.

Becoming aware of the loss

In the first few weeks after the passing, the event still doesn't seem real. It feels as if you are just floating through time, and the numbness is slowly wearing off. During this time, you might start getting stomach pangs as the comprehension of the enormity of what has just happened starts to sink in, and become your reality.

At this stage, pretty much all you can think about is the loss of your parent. It occupies your thoughts constantly. During the first few months after the death, is when one might question oneself whether this event could have been prevented. Reliving the events just up to the death, over and over is also common, as one tries to make rational sense out of something that seems so irrational.

Accepting the reality of the loss

Accepting the reality that your father will never be returning to you, or will never be able to talk to you again is part of the acceptance phase of loss. For a while, there might be a denial of the actual passing of a parent. Until there is an acceptance that the parent is never coming back, a reluctance to acknowledge the death, will slow down the transition through the mourning phase.

At my father's funeral, as I stared at the coffin, I did not believe that he was inside that small box. As I was not allowed to look at his body, it was as if I would never truly know if he had died or not. This took several months for me to accept, and I kept thinking about the box, and about how he looked in there. When the coffin was lowered into the ground, it still did not seem as if he was in there, or if he was, perhaps he was still alive. I knew this was just a delusion to keep me from facing the reality of his death. I didn't want to accept that he was inside there, and not around the corner, waiting for me with a smile on his face.

Becoming aware of our own approaching death

Losing a parent, triggers the fear that we could be next in line. Following the natural path of our parents, we are now no longer immune to death, as somehow we had believed. Until you have experienced the first loss of a parent, could be mother or father, nothing prepares for what you are about to experience. Death seems to be so much closer when the generation above us has gone. This realization is another reason why we react so strongly to the loss of a parent.

Intense Sadness is normal after a loss

Once you are aware of the severity of your personal loss, the feelings of intense sadness is normal. Just remember to experience this intense sadness, is actually helpful to your grieving process, even though it does not feel that way at the time.

What influences the Grieving Period

There are different types of influences on the grief that people experience, when mourning the loss of a parent. Nothing truly prepares us for what we will experience during this period. No one really needs advice, as they will progress at their own pace. However, it can be helpful to know about these influences. The following factors contribute to the length and intensity of the grieving period.

- Type of relationship with the parent will influence the intensity of the grief experience. If you had a very close relationship, and greatly admired and respected the parent, indeed the loss with be more drawn out and all-consuming. If there were unresolved issues with a parent, the grief becomes more intricate and complicated. It might well be advisable to discuss the issues with a professional.
- Cultural background. Certain cultures allow a specific time for mourning, amidst other traditions. When that period has passed, it is time to move on and say goodbye forever.
- Religious backgrounds will affect the time and tradition of bereavement. Many different religions look at death in a different way and the funeral practices and mourning vary widely. For example, Buddhists believe in reincarnation, while Catholics believe in heaven and hell. Hindus cover all religious pictures in the house and do not attend any celebrations for a specific period of time. In Judaism, the mirrors in the house are covered, so the mourners cannot see themselves in a time of intense grief. These are just a few of the very many examples of religious differences.
- A support group can be very influential to the healing process. Family members and friends, who are around to ease the burden of preparing meals, listening, empathizing and providing comfort can greatly affect the length of the grieving period. Without a support system, emotions are harder to deal with, and might get stifled, only to resurface at a later stage.
- Avoiding dealing with the issues by filling time with excessive hours of work, drugs or alcohol, or other compulsive, obsessive or distracting behavior.
- Overuse of prescription drugs such as sleeping pills or self medicating to not have to feel the pain. This will also stifle the grief only to have it reappear at a later stage.

The varied reactions of the healing period

Recovering from the event of the death of a parent, can be a time that one might start to experience stagnation, deterioration or lack of growth in one's life. Everyone handles losing a parent differently. For the most part, people decide that after the mourning period, that it's time for change in their lives, and mostly, it's time to start living. Healing is a slow process, one that can't be rushed.

Did you ever play the game "Red Rover, Red Rover, Let me cross over" when you were a child, and you had to break through a line of kids all holding hands, to get through to the other side? You could use that analogy to understand that the only way to truly heal is to break through the grief by the process of mourning, and acknowledging your loss. Grief is not an emotion that can be skipped, ignored, or unacknowledged. *The only way to truly get through grief is to work through it in whichever method works for you.* Grief is not an easy process to break through. You might get stuck for a while. You may not want to go back to work, or perhaps prefer to isolate at home, thereby not wanting to have to face people, who might inquire about your loss.

In my opinion, the best possible way to get through the grief is to mourn with others who understand what it is you're going through. To actually have to acknowledge your loss, and discuss your feelings, and most of all cry. Every tear brings you closer to healing. Although it doesn't feel like the pain of the loss will ever end, it does. It subsides quietly without you even thinking about it, and suddenly one day, you find yourself enjoying a laugh with a friend, or an event with family. It doesn't mean you're a bad person for not staying sad, it just means that you are healing and working your way through the grief.

How long the pain will last

It would be nice if we knew it would last a specific amount of time like exactly 2 months, 12 days and 3 hours, but in reality, it is different for everyone. Some theorize it takes a year, others 5 years. There is no specific time. You never get over losing the parent that you adored and looked up to. You feel better, and you continue on with your life, but you never ever forget. There is no real specific time for healing, but there is a definite road to recovering and leading a normal life. It's all based upon how you feel and when you are ready. You will know when the pain is diminishing when you feel that your life is gradually returning to normal as you start participating in the activities you enjoy.

The best possible solution is actively making a plan to acknowledge and deal directly with your pain. Don't take advice from others, or have expectations on how long your own personal grieving period should last. The more determined you are to address and resolve your grief, the faster it will subside. When you start feeling like you really want to live life to the fullest, you are well on the road to recovery.

Taking care of yourself

It's important to understand the devastating effects of grief on our bodies. It's also vital that you take care of yourself during the mourning process by any of the following ways.

- Find the time and different ways to relax and contemplate your loss. This includes allowing yourself time to sit quietly and meditate on your own.
- If your home is chaotic, take the time to go somewhere where it's calm and peaceful.

- Allow yourself to mourn, without putting a time limit on your grief.
- Understand that you will go through despair and pine for your parent, and that the longing to see them just one more time never really goes away.
- Get plenty of rest.
- Eat healthy food and drink plenty of water.
- Take nutrients if necessary.
- Keep your life simple and uncluttered.
- Get outside counseling, or join a support group.
- Make an effort to meet people for coffee and a chat.
- Be with your family and people you find comfort with.
- Try to exercise even if you don't feel like it.
- Try prayer
- Try talking out loud to your father, and tell him how you feel.
- Don't put pressure on yourself to do anything, especially in the beginning, as this can be very stressful.

I don't remember much of the first month after my father passed away as everything about that time seems foggy. I remember not leaving the house much, struggling to connect with others, and most of all, wondering what the point of my own existence was. A part of me wished my dad had taken me with him. I felt sure I'd be having a better time over on the other side than here. The worst part for me was mourning on my own. I did not understand the experience I was going through, never having mourned for anyone before. I felt completely distanced and alienated from my family who all were 14000 miles away, and it felt that no-one cared about what I was going through.
I would sit in the garage with the doors closed, and the car running, and wonder how long it would take for me to fall asleep.

I knew inherently that was something I would never consider seriously, because I know it's against the agreements made before I incarnated into this life. Taking my life was not an option, so I had to find another way.

Somehow I knew that there had to be others out there who felt the same way I did, and I started slowly scouring the internet for people going through grief and bereavement. It just so happened that there was a hospice group a mere two blocks from where I live, which welcomed me with open arms. After two private sessions, I joined a nine week group, and suddenly then, I found the people that "got me", that not only understood what I was going through, but were going through the same journey themselves. If it wasn't for this experience, and my desire to understand this somewhat hidden process of grieving the loss of a parent, I would be in a very different place today.

Adjusting to a different environment

Once the funeral is over, the task is left for the family members to deal with the belongings of the deceased parent. There now needs to be an adjustment to the environment without the deceased in it. Everyone has to get used to the emptiness of the house devoid of the presence of one's parent. There might be many memories of the deceased associated to certain items, such as a favorite chair, or a favorite television show that they used to love. The sadness of these memories will be overcome eventually. In the beginning, all items associated with the deceased can be quite overwhelming. As time goes by, the favored items will no longer cause intense grief by the mere observation of them. You do build up a tolerance over time for sentimental items associated with your parent. Make a special place for any sentimental items you have, and on special occasions, take them out in remembrance.

5 THE FAMILY RELATIONSHIPS

There are things that we don't want to happen but have to accept, things we don't want to know but have to learn, and people we can't live without but have to let go.

Author Unknown

I honestly believe that if my father had been present at the table two days after his funeral, things would have been very different. My father's death changed the dynamics and the relationships of myself and my family immensely. It felt like the structure and very fabric of our family changed without his influence in it. I personally found it disturbing that my family were cracking jokes as a way to cope with the loss of my father, however I now understand that this is one of the many ways that people do cope with grief.

Although it is fully expected during our lives that one day we will lose our father, when the moment actually arrives it's unlike anything you have ever prepared yourself for. The different reactions you go through are nothing like how you had envisioned yourself handling one of the most tragic events of your life.

Once the funeral is over, and the noise of the consolers has died away, the family moves onto the details of moving forward with their lives, completing the financial affairs of the estate and other duties and responsibilities of the deceased. This is often not a harmonious time, as there could be varying degrees of agreement on how things should be done, depending on the size of the family.

When this should be a time of healing and reconciliation, it can often lead to devastation of family relationships. As each person within a family handles grief differently, it's important to realize that everyone grieves and heals at their own pace.

Some of the family members immediately go back to deal with their lives while others stay behind to complete their assigned roles, and comfort the remaining parent. The following describes the various issues that could affect relations between family members.

Who to Blame

Be very careful of the feeling that someone is to blame for a parent's death. If there is someone to blame, then that is a whole different story. However, if your parent died naturally, and you feel somehow it was unfair, or you've been somehow cheated, realize that this is just part of the mourning process. Sometimes in the misery, we so badly want to blame someone for why we feel so bad. Recognize this feeling and understand it. It is natural and normal to be angry or miserable and somehow make someone else responsible for this terrible loss you are experiencing. When you are feeling that someone is to blame, be careful of placing that blame on someone else or others, like family members. It's easy to find fault with others when one feels bad, and also in this emotional state to point out faults. Try to distract yourself into a different emotion. Understand by realizing this inclination to blame others is merely part of the grieving process. Try to stay away from the blame game. If something makes you angry, try to walk away from the situation and come back when you've had time to think things through. This is especially important during family communications during this bereavement period. Know that, for the most part, everyone is doing the best they can to cope with their own feelings. Try not to judge or blame, while taking responsibility for your own role in the family.

What affects relationships between family members

- The relationship of those family members to each other and to the deceased. This would include accounting for unresolved issues and disputes between family members.
- Financial resources of family members: This is indicated by how importantly the death will affect the family members future financial resources, as to how actively they wish to participate in the family's financial affairs.
- Sibling rivalry and competitiveness: This can come up with large families such as mine, where there was always a competition for the affection, recognition and acceptance from our parents. Therefore the sibling who perceived their affinity with the deceased as more than others in the family would possibly grieve and lament their loss more.
- Although a family might all experience a commonality in the loss, each might experience the loss in a different way. The members of a family might find it easier to grieve apart than to grieve together as the reminder of the deceased is stronger when looking at other family members.

- Family members might experience anger as well as sadness and grief, and that anger can be directed at other family members for their part or lack of, in the affairs of the deceased parent.
- As children get older, and their parents get frailer, the roles of caring reverse. With this reversal come the changing of the authorative figures. The relationships between family members change, especially with older siblings (over the age of forty), and with the loss of the head figure, new leadership of the family will emerge. This indicates the changing of the authority of two generations. It's at this stage, that existing relationships might break and family members go their own separate ways upon disagreements.

Working Through The Issues

One of the ways to work through these family issues, is acceptance of the loss with all family members involved. In the cases where there are divorced parents and step families, it's important not to push any family members away from important family decisions. Step families and original blood families all feel the same sense of loss, however there may be a distancing after the passing, as the deceased parent may have been the bond that held the family together.

The difference in how men and women grieve

It's important to note the differences in how men and women grieve. Women are naturally nurturing and expressive in a much larger way than men are. Men have been raised with statements such as "Big boys don't cry". This makes it intensely hard to then be able to grieve in public. It has been noticed in various bereavement studies that many men cry in their cars when they are alone. Women also cry in their cars while driving, and in front of others. So within a family, the male members might not cry to show too much emotion beyond their comfort level, while it is acceptable socially for the women to openly cry. Women prefer to discuss their feelings with others, while men will keep themselves busy with work or other time and thought consuming activities.

Family members grieve in different ways

Everyone in the family may have a different way of mourning. It might be uncomfortable to even bring up the topic, as everyone wants to move on and forget about the grief that they are feeling. It's a good idea to create a project which involves the family, to unite the members to remember the great things about the parent who has passed. It's fine to talk about the parent and remember funny events.

The more the loss is discussed, the sooner the family can be of support to one another. Death can unite or destroy families. There can be differences of opinions, blame, anger and discord. There can also be regret of past behaviors towards each other, and renewed commitments to try improve relationships between the siblings and remaining family. Family members can also trigger grief in each other. One member may be perfectly functioning, then when seeing the grief of another, can be triggered back into grieving. The feeling of "Life will never be the same", is true. It never will. However, that doesn't mean it can't be better.

The role of anger in grief

Anger is very normal during the grieving process. There is a propensity to want to blame someone for the loss you are experiencing. Instead of lashing out at others, which is easy to do, there needs to be a constructive channeling of anger. This period of anger can be very disruptive to other family members, and the structure of the family itself. Disagreements can turn into arguments, which can deeply affect family relationships after the loss of a parent. The people in life that we end up not getting along with, are usually those who are closest to us. Hidden feelings of resentment between family members can emerge during the emotions of grief after a parent has passed. This is the time when families can either heal, or seriously self destruct, based on the existing dynamics.

Changing Roles in the Family

The death of the head of the family, brings a change in responsibilities, as well as tremendous upheaval in the family unit. A new leader needs to be appointed. Just like any organizational unit, when the head of the organization is gone, someone else needs to step up and assume responsibilities. In a family unit, it could be the remaining parent, or the older siblings (if there are more than one). Your parent may have left someone in charge of family affairs and that decision needs to be respected. Unity of the family is critical, when attending to the final affairs of the deceased parent. Everything that one's father had responsibility to do, will need to be assumed by another member in the family.

6 TWO MONTHS LATER

He who would learn to fly one day must first learn to stand and walk and run and climb and dance; one cannot fly into flying.

Friedrich Nietzsche

After two months, I am still feeling out of sorts with my body. I constantly ache and feel queasy. It's really hard to move on with my life. My stomach hurts from the unexpected bursts of sadness. I've dropped 10 pounds, and still seem to be losing weight. I guess this is more a result of just not being interested in food, even the good stuff like ice cream, bread and other comfort food does not interest me.

Something innocuous such as picking up photos of my dad with a happy smile on his face, brings out sudden flashes of grief, that briefly completely consume me. I see a picture of my dad standing next to a brand new red corvette I bought in the nineties, and remember an argument I had had with him about a smudge on it. He had loved to clean it, and one time I saw a permanent smudge on the car, and asked him about it. Although I didn't accuse him of making the mark, he took it that way and angrily said he would never wipe down my car for me again. As I looked at the photo of him standing next to this car, I sobbed and said out loud how very sorry I was for accusing him of that, and how much I wished I could take that back. It was just a stupid incident that we both moved on from, and he did still wipe down my car for me after that. For the last few years of his life, every time I visited him, I

always washed and detailed his cars for him. I hope he knew it
was my way of showing him how much I loved him.
Two months after my father's passing, I'm still grieving at
unexplainable times. There are occasions I think I'm getting way
better, only to be submerged and consumed suddenly and
unexpectedly by helpless grief. I'm still angry and powerless, and
the fact that the only people I can discuss any type of feelings
with is a group of strangers in a bereavement group, is upsetting
to me. I feel alienated from my family, and my mother doesn't
realize the amount I am grieving, even though I call her every
single day. I find it hard to really let my feelings show in the
group and find myself making my sharing into something
profound, but in the end, it's all about honesty and real emotions

Healing from grief

So the question is, how do we start healing from grief. Grief is work that takes tremendous emotional and physical toll on one's life. It's an exhausting emotion, and even the smallest of tasks can seem like a major ordeal.

My father had a great saying which I followed for most of my life, and it went like this: "Inch by inch is a cinch, Yard by yard is hard". In other words, you take on the grief one day at a time, without projecting so far into the future that it seems overwhelming.

The majority of people around you are not aware that you are in mourning, especially in the first two months. They expect your normal life to resume after two weeks (after three days if they are your employer). So time needs to be delegated to allow the natural progress through grief and mourning. Society is judgmental about our grief, imposing what it thinks is politically correct as regards to timing. In reality, this politically correctness is nowhere near what really is correct. Be aware of this and understand that most people just do not know how to react or how you really feel. Most people can be very uncomfortable around people who have gone through the loss of a parent, and just don't know what to do. You can help them by telling them to just allow you to talk about your parent without them feeling uncomfortable, and to touch base with you, as its always comforting to know that someone cares.

One loss can trigger others

Many times, when we experience a loss, such as the end of a relationship, divorce, loss of a job, a pet or a loved one, we may not fully comprehend the loss until the next major loss occurs. Then, the summary of all the losses can be connected into the grieving of the most major recent loss. Huge losses may bring to the surface many smaller losses, and the grieving period can be affected by these as well. The most important part of any loss is to find the meaning of it. From the moment we are born, we are setup to experience losses. Whether it be separation from our parents on our first day of school, saying goodbye to college friends, changing or losing jobs, ending relationships, losing friends and family, even pets to death, these are all losses throughout our lives. All these losses have meaning and teach us about the significance of our lives, and our journey here with the rest of the human race.

Setbacks in the mourning process

Even though some time has passed since the actual death of one's parent, and it feels like healing is taking place, there will always be setbacks. There is no clear-cut path that moves directly forward without some bumps in the road. Many times people state they are feeling fine when suddenly something reminds them of their parent, and they are right back in the moment of grief and pain that they were at the time of the death. The grief experienced on one of these setbacks is very real and hurts just as badly as it did before. The difference is the grief subsides faster than it did before. This is an important aspect to understand about the mourning process. You may be in the shower and sudden thoughts come to you about your parent, and you start sobbing. Let those tears come, and when they subside, you will find yourself going about your business again.

I remember being in my car on my way to a business meeting, and I started thinking about my father. The familiar choking in my throat started and my eyes started filling with tears. Out loud I said "Not now Dad, I will cry for you later. I need to be composed for this meeting." With that promise, I composed myself, prevented my makeup from smearing, and carried on with the day. I did indeed keep my promise, and cried later.

These bouts of grief become less frequent, although not necessarily less intense, in the first few months. In time, the intensity will slowly subside as well. When you have researched grief and understand what transitory grief is, that there is an end in sight, you will understand that the bouts of grief that return are just temporary.

As time goes by, you'll be able to talk about your father to others without becoming sad. There will always be a hint of wistfulness, but that's normal, because your father was your whole world at the beginning of your life. As he held you in his arms, you were safe and protected against the world. As you grew and distanced yourself, and became independent, he remained your rock, even from a distance. So yes, the loss is major, no matter what others say. The time will come when people who judged your recovery will go through their own loss, and will finally be able to understand why the grieving process was so difficult for you.

Getting through Fathers day and the holidays

This is one of the biggest fears of mourners. How will they possibly make it through Thanksgiving, Christmas, birthdays and anniversaries and Father's Day. The answer is this, that you just do the best that you can, without pressure from others. If it's too hurtful to be go to a certain place which will remind you of your loss, then for now, stay away from it. Getting together with family members may not be as bad as you anticipated it to be. If you are the one who does the cooking or other responsibilities for the occasion, and you don't feel you can cope, then assign the responsibility to someone else. If you are the one who always hosts Thanksgiving at your house, and you don't feel up to it, ask another member of the family to be the host.

My first Father's Day was incredibly difficult. I took the few precious things I had of my father, his sweater, pen, and handkerchief and laid them out on the bed. I then made a video in which I lit a candle for him and pointed out the significance of each item I had laid out with a brief story, and finished up telling my dad how much I loved him and missed him. Even though 11 months had passed since his death, it was still a very emotional day, and I spent a large part of it crying. I also went online, where I saw others mourning their loss of their father, pretty much going through the same emotions as I was.

How to know that you are starting to recover

As the grief slowly starts to diminish, and one starts to assimilate back into normal life, this is the road to recovery. The ability to hear music that would trigger memories, or go to places, or see people that were part of one's parents life, will be less and less traumatic. One will start to feel re-energized, and look forward with enthusiasm to the future. Plans might be made for vacations, and new careers might be considered. A renewed interest in life and living occurs. When less focus is being placed on the deceased parent, and more focus is on other activities is experienced, then the road to recovery is being well travelled by you.

The intensity of the grief

Soon after the passing of a parent, the intensity of the grief is at the strongest it will be. As time goes by, the intensity and duration of the grief will shorten. This is the normal process of bereavement after the loss of a parent. Everyone grieves in a different way, which is why there is no definitive answer to the question "How long will this grieving period last". The intensity and duration of the grieving period vary according to the type of relationship had, the way the death occurred and if the loss was expected or not. As time goes by, the intensity lessens. Each time you experience the grief, it still feels bad, but just a little less intense. You might consider discussing the feelings of grief with someone you know recently lost their parent. It's very likely that their story will help you with their journey. Often they will relate to your journey through grief, and tell how they felt at the time.

When to seek help

There are times in grieving when going through the normal motions of bereavement just don't work in helping one cope. When certain signs of mourning are just not subsiding, or other unhelpful behaviors are apparent and significant, that may be the time to consider seeking professional help. Some of the signs of these behaviors are:

- Excessive yearning to see the deceased parent again, and focusing solely on the loss.

- Feelings of guilt and blame about something you could have done to prevent the death.
- Wishing you died with them.
- Wishing you had died instead of them.
- Extended periods of depression with suicidal thoughts.
- Inability to function in society or find purpose in living.
- Not wanting to leave the house after several months have passed.
- Not wanting to return to work.
- Not wanting to get out of bed because of insomnia or sleeping too much.
- Overuse of prescription medications and/or drugs.
- Inability to perform normal functions.
- Extreme and continuous weight gain or loss.
- Physical health problems start occurring.
- Inability to recover from the loss.

The mourning process for loss of a parent is a profound experience. The ability to grieve the loss, then move on, without ever forgetting your father, is a difficult process. It's okay to seek help from others, especially professionals in the field. There are many people in the medical profession that spend their careers helping others get through losses of loved one. These bereavement and grief counselors are easy to find, through the internet, or local hospice services, or even through a referral from your local doctor or hospital. Remember, broken hearts isn't just a figurative statement. You can cause real damage to your body by not taking care of yourself

Don't be ashamed of what you are going through. Don't be embarrassed to cry. It would be unusual if you didn't. Seek help if you find it necessary to. It could make a huge difference in your life. There's no reason for you to go through one of the worst experiences of your life on your own, suffering behind closed doors. You have lost one of the most important people in your life, and experienced the most major loss of all, the loss of a father. It takes a lot of courage to work through grief, so be kind to yourself, and forgive yourself for setbacks.

Why bereavement groups can be so helpful

Bereavement groups are a wonderful way to work through mourning the loss of a parent, and regain your sense of purpose in the world. Especially when all your friends have moved on with their own lives, and you feel lost. In these groups you will be surrounded by others who feel exactly the same way. The extreme loneliness of mourning is lessened as you are able to discuss your feelings and thoughts with others.

When you are in a period of mourning, it truly feels like you are all alone and no-one understands your particular grief. A bereavement group will dispel the notion that no-one understands. In the group, you will hear people share about so many things that you can relate to. While the regular world keeps on turning, and you feel like you can't jump on that merry go round, in the group you will feel safe about opening up your feeling and acknowledging your loss. It's not unusual to feel like you have been abandoned or somehow rejected by the rest of the world. The group will be a safe haven that will prepare you for your trip back into the rest of your life. Even just sitting quietly and listening to others will help. Soon you will find yourself wanting to join in and share. You will also make new friends with whom you may want to meet up with every so often when the group ends.

I highly recommend this if possible. Look at the local hospices for these groups and I'm sure you will find one relatively close to you.

Making life-changing decisions

While going through the bereavement period, *it's important not to make any life-changing decisions,* such as finding a new job, moving to a new town, ending a relationship, or anything else that would normally be viewed as an impulsive move under normal circumstances. It's a good idea to let enough time pass so that whatever decisions are made are ones that are solidly thought out. The death of a parent can bring on thoughts of ending old habits and starting out fresh on new adventures, and making our lives more fulfilling. Suddenly, the fragility of life is experienced and realized. When confronted with a parent's death, we are confronted with the prospect of our own passing one day. There is a sense of there only being a limited amount of time left in our lives, so we better "live it up" while we can. These feelings are fine, as long as the actions we take are not harmful, or hurtful to ourselves or others in the long run.

Ask yourself before making any decision "What would my father have advised me to do? Is this a good idea, or am I rushing things based upon how I feel?" If you can honestly answer those questions from a non-emotional viewpoint, then proceed. Take time with every decision you make. Write out pros and cons with the intent of making a sound decision. The reason to carefully think things through is to avoid making mistakes we will regret at a later time. Bounce the ideas off someone who is less emotionally involved.

The same concept goes for throwing out your parent's clothing immediately after their passing. Why not wait until you feel ready to do so? Keep in mind, what you throw away in haste may have been cherished by others. Take your time, and slowly move through the process.

7 GRIEVING AND SOCIAL MEDIA

Social networks aren't about Web sites. They're about experiences

Mike DiLorenzo

When I was in some of my darkest moments of grief and mourning, I discovered the internet was full of people just like me. Going through exactly what I was. I used Google to research grieving sites, Facebook to express my grief the day I found out my father had passed away, and You-tube to create a Father's Day commemoration.

Who knew that someday a chapter in a book would be called *grieving and the social media*? I certainly didn't. Until I lost my father, I never even had considered the possibility of web sites being out there to console and comfort people mourning the loss of their loved ones. How fortunate we are that we live in an information age, where information about any topic is so readily available. Even twenty years ago, you had to go to a bookstore to try and find the topic of your choice. Today, we can access that information merely by turning on our computer and clicking on a link. Not only are there so many people suffering, just as you or I are, but there are also many congruencies between how people are moving through the grieving process.

Social media has become a public place to express your grief. These online sites record people's feelings and emotions and are good reminders of how we are all united in our losses, and that we're not the only ones grieving. Social media have become so mainstream in our lives, that it's something that needs to be acknowledged by the medical profession. It's no longer unusual to see a memorial page or a RIP statement among Twitterers and Facebook friends. Events that happen can be instantly broadcast due to social media, so that within minutes people are informed. When a death is announced, or an anniversary of a death, it enables others to share their stories of loss as well, and provides comfort to knowing one isn't going through this tragic event alone. Social media provide an outlet for grief and bereavement larger than anything else has in history. Pages are created honoring people's lives after death. and allowing others to contribute their personal stories and experiences as well as having an outlet to mourn. It seems that mourners find it easier to put their grief into words in writing or blogging online than to actually talk to someone in person.

There are many similar sites where one can express one's grief. There are many opportunities for communication on the internet that you can use to your advantage, and can be a useful tool in grieving.

One of the favorite websites that I found was Imissmydad.com. I was so elated that I had found a place where people were actually expressing their grief, suffering and emotions that I could relate to. Not only was this a place where I could read other people's experiences, but I could give comments, offer condolences and put my own experiences out there, too.

What I found interesting and inspirational is that the people who posted on these sites wrote from the perspective of speaking directly with their dads. I immediately emailed the owner of the site, told him I was writing a book, and he very kindly agreed to let me include some of the commentaries on his site. Here are some of the posts given with permission from the website owner of www.missmydad.com.

Give you hope and courage

My Dear Dad, I tried to give you hope and courage throughout your suffering. You believed in me and my strength and fought the worst battle. Not once did I shed a tear in front of you, because I feared it would scare you. If you only knew how many times I wanted to throw my arms around you and just cry. To show you just how scared I was of losing you. There has not been one day throughout the past year, since you have left this earth, that I have not shed a tear for you. I miss you so much Daddy! I wish I had spent more time with you when you were well. I know you know I was always there for you till the end. But somehow that is just not good enough for me. I wish I had told you how sorry I was for all those days you wanted to spend time with me and I always had an excuse. I wish I had those happy memories as a child all back again. I would do so many things differently. Yesterday was my 40th birthday and if someone would have told me years ago that I would be celebrating it without you, I never would have believed them. You gave me life and all your love. I can never thank you enough for everything you ever did for me. I just wish you were still hear with us all. Love your daughter Margaret.

Wasn't ready for you to go

I love you daddy. I wasn't quite ready for you to go yet. I knew it was coming because of your leukemia, but I wasn't ready for you to go in only a couple months, surely not 5 days before Christmas. I learned a lot of things from you in our time together, my favorite was to treat each day like Christmas, celebrating the birth of Christ and his teachings every day. I am proud of you dad, you were a good man, and always stayed strong, you taught me that. Even now, when I am hurting deep inside, I will be strong, cause I know you are in a better place now and that you will be there when my time comes to lead me by my hand, to be with God. I don't know how I'll stop grieving, but I do know, that I must forge ahead, cause you would have wanted me to. I know you are watching over me now, and I know you will always be with me, and that comforts me some. I love you daddy, and I am grateful I am your daughter. Love Always, your daughter, Michele

I am a Doctor. I don't cry

My father died 4 weeks ago. I haven't cried. I don't understand. I loved him very much and we had a good relationship. He was a doctor. I am a doctor. Even while I write this I don't feel anything, yet ten years ago, a beloved pet died and it dropped me to my knees. While he was going through his illness, he would ask me, "What do I have?" I would tell him, "End-state renal disease." He would then say, "What does that mean?" I would tell him, "Dad, I know what it means, I'm a doctor too." He prepared me all my life for his death. He prepared everyone around him, including my mother, for his death. At the funeral, the remark was made, "You women are really strong." My sister, myself and my mother didn't cry. We're talking about a man that was loved tremendously. The funeral director said that seeing our family made it worthwhile to come to work--that he could tell that my father was loved. I even sang and played the guitar at the gravesite in celebration of his life. He loved and played music. But still I don't cry. There are times that I tear up, but I get past it. I know this isn't a normal way of grieving. I know I'm not in denial of his death. He made it known that he wanted someone to make sure that he was really dead after they pronounced him dead. I checked his pulses, one hour post mortem, just because he wanted me to. There was no doubt in my mind that he was dead. The only thing I can think of, about my inability to cry, is that he talked to me clinically from the beginning of his illness. He didn't have anyone else in the family that he could talk to clinically about his health, on that level, except for me. He was scared and I was his confidante. Clinicians don't cry, they manage health care. Those talks with my father, coupled with the fact that my father told me many times, "Doctors don't cry," could be the reason that I don't. Dad, this doctor needs to.

Grieving on Facebook

Over the last several years, Facebook, the social network site which was launched in 2004, has become a huge example of how social media has changed our lives. With almost 750 million (at the time of this writing) users worldwide, it has become the single most common way to broadcast news and keep in touch with your friends and family with a quick post. Social media has changed the way we deal with mourning and grief. Facebook has become a new reality for those of us grieving the loss of a loved one.

The day I heard my father had passed, I posted the following to Facebook.

Contrary to anything I've said before, today is actually the worst day of my life. My darling father Siggy passed away yesterday, and

I was too late to say goodbye, and I don't think my life will ever be the same. RIP Dad, I love you and will always miss you!

Thirty people responded to me within about 24 hours, and it was a great way for me to not only put my grief out there as an emotional outlet, but to have others acknowledge my grief. Even if the people who you would like to acknowledge your suffering don't respond, there will be others that do support you. The world is actually now better connected than it ever was before, and social media sites like Twitter and Facebook can give you a huge circle of support.

When going through intense grief, it can feel like an ordeal to rejoin society after the funeral is over. There's a loneliness that can't be resolved by people being around you. It's almost like a journey into a long dark tunnel that one needs to move through, with the light at the end being the ability to lead a normal life again.

Here are some Facebook pages on grief

Type in the word 'grief' or "bereavement' in the search bar to see many more examples of memorial or grief pages. Each page below has a different name even though they look similar. Here are some of my favorites:
- Finding Hope in Times of Grief
- Grief Loss & Recovery
- Writing Through your Grief
- Hello Grief
- Bereavement in Online Communities Project
- You may have died, but I love and remember you - R.I.P
- I Miss My Dad...
- I miss my dad :'(
- I MISS YOU A LOT DAD !!
- I Miss My Dad And Love My Dad

- **I Miss My Dad.com**

Here is an excerpt from the Facebook 'I miss my dad' page.

Not a minute goes by that I don't think about you

Dad- It's been 13 weeks since the accident, not a minute goes by that I don't think about you. In the newspaper tonight there were pictures of everyone that attended your 50th high school reunion. You were so excited to attend it this year! At your calling hours one of your classmates told me that you were the 81st person to pass away from your class. How sad. My heart is broken, Dad....I just want you back so bad. I want to be your little girl again. There are so many things that we didn't do, so many conversations that we never had....I love you, Dad

And another...with the corresponding comments

PJ: Today is 5 months since my Dad passed away..I am in so much pain from his loss..it seems to be getting harder for me...I joined a bereavement group and I am hoping it will help a bit..RIP my Beautiful Dad! ♥

CA: For a while you do anything to keep going. I went on anti depressants about 4 months after losing my Dad (I lost him 40 days after losing my Mom) and now.. after a year and 8 months, I am trying to see if I can do it without the meds. I notice I seem to be on the verge of tears a lot more. Good luck with the bereavement group, and know it does get better. It's with you all the time, but after a while, it just becomes part of you, and not the knife in your heart that you have right now. I promise.

PJ: CA thank you so much for your comforting thoughts..you said it perfectly when you said "it's with you all the time, but after a while it becomes a part of you ,not the knife in your heart"...so true! I lost my mom when I was 16,so I know it does get somewhat easier from that knife in your heart feeling..again thanks :)... sorry for your loss of your Parents

CA: Omg at 16, I am so sorry. Mom's are hard, but daddy's and daughters.. oh Lord. I hope my words help, t his group helped me a lot when I first joined, now I visit here and there on more difficult days, instead of daily.. I guess we are a work in progress, eh?

PJ: we sure are, my friend! :)

CH: It's been almost two years since I lost my daddy...and I know how you feel, because it has never gotten any easier...the days seem to drag when all I want to do is talk to him. Just make sure that you give yourself the chance to grieve...and that it's ok.

As you can see from the above conversation after the initial post, the writer's feelings and emotions are validated. *Even though the validation comes from people unknown to the writer, a feeling of empathy is conveyed by someone who has experienced the same devastating type of loss. This is a very helpful tool in getting through grief.*

Other places of interest on the web

Here are some more interesting websites to consider:
- livinginspirit.wordpress.com/
- www.ilasting.com/
- www.griefshare.org/
- www.griefnet.org/
- www.ards.org/links/griefhealing/
- www.journeyofhearts.org/
- www.hospicefoundation.org
- www.aarp.org/relationships/grief-loss/
- www.webhealing.com/
- www.bereavement-poems-articles.com/

A website like forevermissed.com will allow you to build a memorial page to your loved one (for a fee, of course), but sites like Facebook and Twitter are free.

If you happen to be among the older generation of people who have not been exposed to these sites, then start with the above sites as a place where to look. There are many who are not as computer savvy as others, and would find great benefit by utilizing these resources online.

So, venture into the online world and utilize these social media and grieving sites. Not only will you feel more connected to the world, and less alone in your grief, but your expression of mourning might help other people have hope, who are going through the same experience as you are. You will find many resources to help you through the grieving process. I've only mentioned a few here, but there are many.

8 WHAT A MIGHTY FINE MAN

I'd like to thank you from the bottom of my heart, and from my wife's bottom too...

Siggy Michelson
(part of any speech on any particular occasion)

This is the chapter where I honor my father, someone who was so important to my life. I hope he knows how much I really loved him, and how special he was to so many people. The above phrase was what he started his speeches with during the many parties he and my mom had.

The Final Tribute

"Some days are Diamonds, Some days are Stones" by John Denver was one of my father's favorite songs. That pretty much epitomized how he led his life, taking on the good and the bad with equal effort. In honor of his life, here are some pictures from the beginning of his journey until the end.

My father was born on March 2nd, 1927, and grew up during the great depression. He loved his parents, especially his father. My father grew up believing you honored your parents, as it says in the ten commandments of the Old Testament.

Here is a picture of him with my grandfather, who died long before I was born. My father got to hold his father's hand when he took his final breath. He didn't want his father to die, just like I didn't want mine to either. How I wish I could have held my father's hand at the end of his life.

Nothing in the human experience changes, except time. My father was once a little boy who adored his daddy, just like you or I did at that age.

He was a very conscientious little boy who was extremely careful with his things. As money was tight, it being the period of the Great Depression, he painstakingly saved every cent that he could. This was a habit that would continue his entire life.

As his parents were from different faiths, his Grandfather on his father's side disinherited his son. When my father was around 3 years old, his parents sent him to knock on the old man's door, while they hid behind the shrubs. When the door opened, this little 3 year old said "Hello Grandpa, I'm Siggy!". Apparently this melted his grandfather's heart, who then made amends with his son, my grandfather.

In this picture, he's the smaller one on the right with a big smile on his face, with his brother. I wonder if someone had told him then, he would grow up, get married and have five children and a lovely long life, what he would have thought about that. (He probably would have cried about the five children part.) This must have been around 1930. It's hard to identify with one's parent being a child once themselves, but once we do, we come to realize it's all part of life's process for everybody, without exclusion.

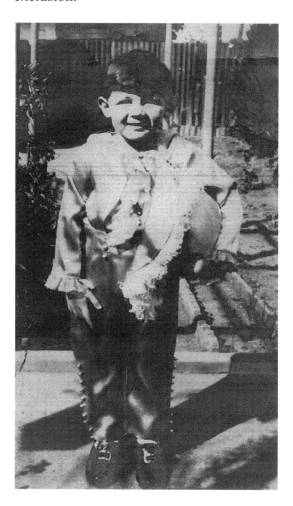

He had his whole life ahead of him. Could he have know how fast 84 years can fly by? Every human being has a journey, and a path to take, which is entirely their own. We all have a part to play, in the drama called life. Whether we're young or old, every single person is special and has a purpose for existence.

At the age of 5, he was a newspaper boy, earning his first salary in 1932.

GREEN & SEA POINT BOYS' HIGH SCHOOL.

30th April, 1945.

Sieghfried Michelson came up from our Junior School at the beginning of 1939. He obtained his Junior Certificate in 1941 and subsequently his Matriculation in February, 1944.

Michelson was a very earest and conscientious student, but he no less participated in all the extra mural activities of the school.

He consistently played Rugby, and Football and was a member of the First Fifteen in 1943. He swam for the School and was awarded his Half Colour. In the School Cadet Corps he was the Drum Major and took part in the Efficiency Competitions. He played Second Violin in the School orchestra.

Michelson was a very good citizen of the school and a boy of many parts. His sterling qualities of character, his popularity with his schoolmates and the high esteem of his Masters earned him the position of a School Prefect. To these qualities he added a sense of responsibility, a very good address, courteous manners, and a charming personality. I have every confidence that Michelson will acquit himself with credit in whatever sphere he moves and win the esteem and respect of those he has to do with.

(Signed) Ronald Graham M.A.

HEADMASTER.

My dad was an avid rugby player and swimmer. He remained friends with a number of his high school buddies for the rest of his life.

He was born just before the Great Depression, and times were hard when he was a teenager. They were poor, and his mother (my grandmother) was very careful and conscientious about how she raised her children. My grandfather loved gambling, especially the horse races; as a result, there were many times when money was scarce. My father remembers only getting one egg for breakfast, and because of that, my mother always had to give him two or more. (Isn't it strange how we take life for granted, when back during hard times like the Great Depression, one extra egg could be considered a luxury and make a difference to someone's life.)

SEA POINT BOYS HIGH SCHOOL
1943

He participated in everything in life with enthusiasm. In the above picture he is a leader of the school band. It was during wartime in 1943 and he was finishing up high school getting ready to join the army.

It was in high school he learned to play the bugle, which he was particularly fond of. Later in his life, at parties, he would happily play it loudly, much for everyone's amusement, and much to the consternation of the neighbors.

Here he was around thirteen years old serving in the boy scouts, walking through the streets of Cape Town.

When my father graduated from high school, he went into the military, getting prepared to join the fight in North Africa. Luckily for all of us, the war ended just before he was to ship out. He did indeed win the esteem and respect of everyone he dealt with during his life.

My parents met at my mom's 21st birthday party. He looked across the room and told his friend he was going to marry her. His friend said "Don't be silly Siggy, have another drink!". My dad agreed, and after that drink he stated that now he knew he was going to marry her. They went on 3 dates, got engaged and married six weeks later, then apparently spent the first year arguing. They worked out their differences that year, and stayed married for the rest of their lives, 59 years. He was 25 years old in this picture.

This is one of my favorite pictures of him. When I think of my dad, this is how I picture him in my head. Not at the age he was when he passed. It's almost like this is how he wants me to remember him, as a man who was young, had dreams and ambitions and is young again on the other side.

My parents on their wedding day. They married very young, he 25 and she 21.

This is another picture on the day of my father's marriage to my mom. They had a glorious wedding in a beautiful setting in the countryside. It was a very glamorous affair, I've been told. They had a love, admiration and respect for each other that lasted right throughout their marriage.

He was a very well-known and respected man. He had so many friends and people that cared about him. When you were the focus of his attention, he made you feel very special. It amazed me, even in the last decade of his life, how many people would show up on a daily basis at my parents home, to say hello and have a chat.

He passed only six months before their 60th anniversary, and his 85th birthday.

This is the last picture I will show of him. I know he would not want me to show pictures of him in his fragile condition at the end of his life. This was taken several years before his death. He was very meticulous about his appearance right throughout his life, and always made an effort to be presentable every day. He was a considerate, amiable and an accommodating man. Very polite and chivalrous, irrespective of the age of the person he was talking to.

The one thing I can say with certainty about my father is that he lived! He enjoyed his life, being with good friends, drinking great wine (cheap or expensive), playing his bugle loudly at midnight, entertaining with a larger than life personality, telling jokes, being charitable, being kind, being determined, ambitious and most of all, living his life with honor, integrity and grace. He truly lived!

So, in conclusion, here was the life of a man who was a husband, a father, a brother, a neighbor and great friend, someone who made a difference. He is deeply mourned and is remembered with love and respect by those who knew him.

Goodbye Dad! As the light fades, and the music of your bugle goes quiet, we honor your life your existence and presence in the world, and wish you well on your journey into the great beyond, where we will meet again someday.

9 THE REMAINING PARENT

"There is only one page left to write on. I will fill it with words of only one syllable. I love. I have loved. I will love."

Audrey Niffenegger, The Time Traveler's Wife

My mother's reaction to the shock of losing my father was to keep herself extremely busy with TV, reading, preparing food and being with her family. Unfortunately, this postponing of dealing with the real emotions behind the shock would definitely catch up with her later, as it did for myself.

There I was, lying on my mother's bed, with my arm around her, unable to provide any comfort other than just being there. When she said "I have nothing left to live for", I replied that she had us children to live for. She said "You all have your own lives", to which I had no reply. I couldn't envision her life ever being the same without my dad.

After 59 years of marriage, never having lived on her own, my mother was now faced with the monumental task of finding a reason to continue her existence. I did not know how to comfort her. I put my arms around her and just let her cry until the tears subsided.
I feel that it's really important to me to be there for her. She's all I have left of my parents and I fear for her going too. My mother told me, that at the time of my father's death, all she felt was complete bewilderment. I didn't know how to protect my mother from her pain. All I wanted to do was stop her hurting somehow,

but that is her path, one that she will have to walk alone. I can hold her hand, but I can't make her walk.

Here in the USA, there are hundreds of thousands of new widows every year. As people get into their sixties and seventies, there are many more widows than widowers. Statistics state that almost half of women over the age of 65 are widowed. Your parent needs to understand that they are not alone in their grief.

The loss of a parent has especially a profound effect on all members of a family. The attention is usually piled onto the grieving widow, and every effort is made to comfort her and make sure she is feeling no pain. This is actually just prolonging the inevitable, as she will have to work through the pain and the loss in her own time.

The children of a family constantly check on the surviving parent, if there is one, and watch their every move, to make sure they are coping. The surviving spouse has to stoically cope in front of family and friends, and might well be concerned about breaking down and crying uncontrollably in front of strangers. In my case, my mother refused to go to the funeral, and sat with two old friends during the event, at my sister's house. Afterwards, in a much more intimate setting, she bravely faced everyone coming up to her saying "Sorry for your loss". This sentiment would then be said to each of the next family members sitting in a row. While much attention is given to the surviving spouse, not as much focus is given to how much the death has affected the surviving family members, especially in a large family such as mine as discussed in previous chapters.

The new beginnings of a widow

The remaining spouse has an uphill battle for the first year after the loss of their spouse. They have many coping skills to learn, new responsibilities to take care of, and most of all, the intense loneliness to deal with. That empty space on the bed is what the remaining spouse faces first thing in the morning, and last thing at night.

As a child, you want to ensure the happiness of your remaining parent, and it is intensely difficult to sit there feeling helpless about how to make them feel better. There is no easy way around grief. There is just a slow methodical forward movement through it.

Sitting at a sidewalk cafe in Antibes in the south of France on a vacation, I observed a woman sitting with her elderly mother. For the hour that I sat there, the woman was on the phone completely ignoring the elderly lady. I knew that one day she would be angry at herself for not making the most of every minute she had left with her mother. Spend time with the remaining parent. There will come a time when you wished you had placed more value on their presence in your life. Don't have regrets about what you could have done with your remaining parent. Make the memories now.

Easy Does It

It's vitally important not to make hastily thought through decisions. Let the first few days go by as stress free for the new widow as possible. Make sure she's comfortable, fed and surrounded by family. There will be plenty of time later for her to be alone, once all the fussing of the funeral arrangements are over. Let her partake in minimal stress activities such as meal planning. The impact of the loss will happen after the noise of the funeral has subsided.

Here are a couple of do's

- Allow time for the remaining parent to process their grief. The initial disbelief and bewilderment of the loss, with the accompanying numbness will wear off and the shock of grief and mourning will then be experienced.
- Reduce as much stress as you can for them, by allowing them time to grieve. Have patience and understanding about your mother's progress at this time. It is a huge loss for her.
- Understand that there will be many different emotions experienced. Age doesn't diminish the emotions. Just because the surviving widow may be in their eighties, it doesn't make it any easier. In fact, in many instances, it might be harder to bear, based on many factors such as the length of time together, intensity of the reliance upon one another for care, comfort and love.
- Acknowledge their grief by listening without judgment to what they have to say. Stay in constant contact. Make a daily call, even if it's just for a few minutes. It makes a huge difference to the one left behind that they are being thought of.
- Be kind and loving to your remaining parent. They looked after you when you were unable to look after yourself, so return the favor.
- Encourage grieving. There's an important step to healing, through grief. Many of our parents did not grow up with "new age" touchy feely positive thinking mantra's and self help books. Our parents grew up with not showing one's emotions on their sleeves, and putting on a brave face for others.

- Purchase a couple of books on coping with the loss of a spouse, and some inspirational stories for the widow. DVD's on the subject matter would be just fine too. The surviving spouse may not want to read it, as it might be too painful.
- Encourage your parent to get spiritual and emotional support outside of the family. If there are any retreats or getaways they can do, it would be tremendously helpful. This will of course depend on the age and agility of the surviving spouse. Many times, there will be a reluctance to do anything. They might inform you that they will get through it in their own way.

Here are a couple of don'ts

- Don't encourage your widowed parent to spend large amounts of money, such as shopping for cars, or other such items to temporarily relieve the grief.
- Don't put the house up for sale. *Death and moving are two of life's most stressful and traumatic events.* Why combine them to make a double whammy for a person grieving their spouse?
- Don't encourage financial risks of any type, without thorough research.
- Don't immediately throw out the deceased's belongings (clothes, shoes, socks, photos and other personal items). This could be greatly regretted later, and is usually done in the heat of the family's emotions. There are items that could be hastily discarded that another family member might treasure.
- Don't immediately move. The unfamiliar surroundings won't be as comfortable as familiar ones. The exception to

this would be if the remaining parent is unable to care for themselves. If your parent is somewhere safe, where the neighbors can check in from time to time, then don't move them and create even more stress. Allow the grief to subside until decisions can be made after careful thought and planning for the future.

- Don't allocate a specific period by which the remaining spouse should now be able to "move on". Just as you have experienced your loss of a parent, imagine how difficult it is for the remaining spouse who deals with the loss every time they look at their bed, when they wake up in the morning, and go to bed at night.
- Don't be impatient with forgetfulness, lack of interest or motivation. This should be expected and is part of the mourning process.

Understand, as hard as it may be, that the remaining parent may not want to live without their spouse. It may be a temporary emotion if they say they have nothing to live for, or it may not be.

Things widows don't like to hear

- "How are you doing?" It's all in the emphasis of the asking. Are you meaning "How are you doing with the suffering?" What a widow would really like to tell you is how bad she's really feeling, as opposed to the expected "I'm doing better, thanks." You more than likely wouldn't like to hear how she really is doing.
- "Let me know if you need anything". This is particularly annoying when heard from many well-meaning people that don't intend on really following through. After all,

how would that person feel about a late night call from the widow during an emotional grieving crisis?

- "He's in a better place". While this may be true, it's not at all comforting to have your emotions about the loss discarded. This is an undermining of the devastating loss of the one left behind.
- "You're welcome to stop by and have dinner with us anytime". Rather call with a specific time in mind, while pretending it's spontaneous. The offer might be declined initially, but as time goes by, they will be very grateful for the invitation.
- "Oh, well he had nice long life". Once again, this is not acknowledging the painful loss of the one left behind. What you're really saying is, "He had a nice long life, you should feel good about that and move on."
- "I know how you feel". Unless someone has personally experienced this, they just don't know. However well intentioned one is, it's better not to say something trite.

Words of encouragement to the widow

Your very foundation has been shaken. You never expected to be on your own. Your partner was such a large portion of your life, and now you have to learn to create a whole new life on your own. This was something you can never prepare for. You are now faced with the task of having your own identity as others saw you a half of a whole. In reality you were always a whole, sharing a life with another. Now you are a whole with your own life still ahead of you. Loss was something that happened to others, and not to you. Expect mood swings and intense periods of grief. It's very normal to also experience anger towards the spouse that left you to face the cruel world alone. Keep in mind, there are so many seniors going through exactly what you are. You are not in this alone. Try to find others who have experienced the same type of loss you have. They will understand and "get" you.

Allow yourself time to grieve and mourn. You need to mourn and say goodbye to your loved one in your own way. Expect the chronic grief, which disturbs your sleep and occurs in unexpected waves. Imagine that grieving is like walking up a steep hill. Eventually you are going to get to the top, where you will then be able to look back with pride to see how far you've come.

Understand that there will always be setbacks, and memories. You will always have the memories of the one you loved, that you can contemplate about when you are alone. When you move through the process, don't feel guilty about enjoying your life or laughter. It doesn't mean you will ever forget your loss. It just means that you are enjoying being alive. It's okay to talk about your loved one, and enjoy the funny memories with laughter. It's okay to have conversations with that person (preferably when you are on your own). There is no wrong and right as it's a one step at a time process, for you to work through your grief. Don't push yourself to do anything or go anywhere, when you are not ready. If you need time out, take that time.

How long will it take to feel normal?

It would be wonderful to have an absolute answer to this (such as 6 months, one year, two years, etc), but unfortunately it varies. People move on to happy productive lives. Some remarry, some find great new friends and interests. You're in a club that no-one really wants to be in, but will find themselves there anyway. You might feel like the skin has been ripped from your body, with the loss of your spouse. The object is to grow a new skin, one that will protect you against the rawness of your loss, and help you moving forward to cope with living again. There is no easy way through grief. To repeat my father's favorite saying "Inch by Inch is a cinch. Yard by Yard is hard". Make little steps, and they will turn into yards.

Keep in mind, when someone dies, they often leave many mourners behind. Commiserate and discuss your feelings with those other family members that are experiencing loss. Talk to someone who understands how you feel. There are many wonderful hospice societies that have special groups for "Loss of a Spouse". You will walk into that room and have instant rapport with everyone there. You will want to talk to everyone, because everyone there "get's it"!

Ask for hugs. You need to be touched. No one survives alone. That's not how we as the human race survive. If you're tired, sleep. If you want to cry, do so. Eat nutritious food and try to stay healthy. Grieving puts immense stress on your body, so try to prepare it for the onslaught. Take care of yourself. Try to exercise or get out of the house every day. Setup a schedule which you can commit to. Get up, bathe and get dressed, even if you are not expecting visitors. Watch comedies and funny movies to get yourself in a brighter mood. Be kind to yourself.

Try meditating, and prayer. If you're religious, recognize the God has special empathy for mourners. In Matthew 5:4 from the New International Version, it says "***Blessed are those who mourn, for they will be comforted.***"

This is about restarting your life after your loss. Some days will be better than others. Join other seniors and try to take part in the community. Keep yourself busy with activities if you can. Isolating is no fun, so reach out to others. Plan fun things with family members. Dying is a part of living, and it's going to happen to all of us without exception, so try to enjoy the time you have left, as it goes by quickly.

10 MESSAGES FROM THE OTHER SIDE

There will be a time when you believe everything is finished.
That will be the beginning.

Louis L' Amour

We are all spiritual, before we are physical.

From the beginning of time, we have all wondered where we come from, and why we are here. We see the miracle of birth, starting from the merging of cells, to the actual birth of a human, who has a soul, a mind and comprehension. We watch the human body grow, mature, and then die, and many of us ponder what happens next. We have all followed the concept that our creation starts at birth. What if that wasn't the beginning of our creation, and we had existed before we were born? If that's the case, then it stands to reason that we are all spiritual, before we become human, or physical.

Emerging from Spiritual to Physical

We are completely reluctant as a race to believe that we were once non-physical beings, part of our Creator, and became separate and physical through the birth process. We incarnate into physical form, and this process is repeated over and over again until we are once more re-united with universal life force that created us. The reason for this, is that we have to advance through many spiritual levels until we reach the highest level to be reunited with God.

What if all the answers to all the questions we have, we already know? What if we were born with that knowledge but just didn't know it? If we knew these things for sure, we would be quiet and really listen to the inner voice inside us, which taps the knowledge from the universe, the knowledge we have always known.

From many writings, dating back thousands of years, people have realized we are indeed more spiritual than we are physical. Before we incarnate into a physical body (which is by our choosing before our birth), we decide on our life's events. Not everything that happens to us is random, or good or bad luck. Not every single event is planned out, but many of the major ones are. We decide on the lessons we need to learn on incarnating into this physical life. We decide who our parents and siblings are, and who will be put into our lives to teach us specific lessons. The relationships closest to us are there for very specific reasons, and when we don't get along with those people, we need to try and figure out what the life lessons are for each specific turbulent relationship. This is a reason why we pick our spouses, even though we may not get along with them, and find ourselves wondering why on earth we would pick that specific person to be married to, and to have to endure such misery in the marriage. Once again, it's a life lesson. There is a lesson to be learned from every one of life's experiences. There is a reason for the good and the bad, happy and sad events of our lives.

When someone is taken from us, at a young age, the lesson is for the people closest to them who are left behind. How will they handle that event, and what kind of person will that lesson turn them into. I know someone who died in his early twenties in a car accident barely a year after his father had passed away. He was the great kid that was the apple of his parent's eyes. He was great at everything he did, good looking, athletic, and an all round very popular guy. His younger brother faded by comparison. After my friend's passing, his younger brother became the man of the family. He grew up, went to college, got a great job, got married and had children of his own. He became the head of the family, taking on all the responsibilities of finances and care for his remaining family. The learning lesson in this particular story was that this was meant to happen, perhaps to teach the lesson of responsibility to the surviving brother. He was unwillingly pushed by circumstances to take the place of the head of the family, and did a fine job, turning into a wonderful family man. I had the pleasure of meeting up with him a few years ago, and was so impressed by the person he had become.

Everything in life that happens, comes about because it is meant to. There are no accidents or coincidences. What we do have is free will to make choices. Don't mistake the choices we have with free will, with the grand life-changing events that we had planned before our existence. For instance you might ask, well what if that friend of yours had made a different choice and not been in the car that he was killed in? The answer is, that he would have then died some other way.

When someone we love ceases to exist, a part of us dies along with them. Being able to communicate with our loved ones after we die is very comforting and healing, and can be productive in helping us move through the grief.

What does everyone do when they get to the other side?

This is a concept that everyone struggles with. What happens to us after we die? What happens to our bodies? Can we still breathe, or eat?

From the many writings of mediums, psychics and philosophers it seems that once we shed our spiritual bodies of our current incarnation, and make the crossing, it is extremely busy over there. The deceased's life gets reviewed, mistakes are reviewed and all our relationships are analyzed, and either the spirit stays with his spirit soul group for a while, or prepares for the next life. We'll discuss re-incarnation in the next chapter,

Why it's important to have a spiritual connection

The understanding and comprehension of a life after death make our mourning process easier, and help us move through the grief. Knowing that our loved one still exists, but only in a different form, gives us hope and peace for the rest of our own existence. Also knowing that someone who has passed is not lost, and is still reachable, changes the whole process of absorbing the loss, and helps us heal faster. Understanding that our loved ones are still with us is extremely important and comforting in getting through the bereavement period. People who have a stronger sense of spirituality adapt much easier to these beliefs, and are open to hearing messages from the other side. Intense mourning and grieving block the messages to an extent, and the more accepting and at peace one is, the easier it is for our loved ones to communicate.

What happens at the time of death

At the time of the passing (according to the many writings of mediums and people who have experienced near death experiences), the soul leaves the body through the crown of the head. The life cord slowly disintegrates over the period of 3 days. The soul is greeted by familiar family members and moves onto a journey into the great beyond. This is what has been reported by many mediums in all parts of the world, who have communicated with those who have passed over.

Quantum physics explains physical reality

Quantum physics has proved that there are dimensions where particles cannot be seen, and that we live in a multi-dimensional cosmos. Quantum mechanics is the quest of understanding of the nature of our physical reality. If we truly understand our physical reality and consciousness, and how everything consists of matter, which in turn is energy, then we should be able to comprehend the possibility of our non-physical reality.

With quantum theory, we can no longer look at the world thinking we are seeing everything that is to be seen. If that's true, then the actuality of a spirit world in a different dimension is not that farfetched, is it? We think of our material world as real, when in actuality, energy and matter is the same thing, therefore everything is energy including us.

Types of communication from the other side

There is an ability for us to communicate on a spiritual level with one another. What is needed is a tuning in, just like on a radio station, to hear from those who have passed on. There are different methods that we can be communicated with from beyond the physical world.

1. *Clairaudience:* This is when you can actually hear a spirit communication in your head. It sounds like you're in a large room, and someone is sitting on the other side of the room talking to you. This is where a psychic can hear voices or sounds. You can actually hear thoughts as if they are spoken out aloud. I actually have this ability, although, the number of messages I have received in my lifetime, I could count on two hands. This can also happen with someone that you are in tune with on a psychic level, when they are still alive. (In my case, while my father was still living, on one particular occasion, I heard his thoughts as if he had actually said something out loud. On other occasions, I would pick up on his feelings, such as anger, fear, etc). Clairaudience is a way of receiving thoughts communicated from another spiritual realm.

2. *Clairvoyance:* In French this means having "Clear sight", which is the ability to see things that are in a different realm, or to remote view them. This is the ability to see beyond the normal range of perception. Famous psychics had this ability, such as Edgar Cayce (Who lived from 1877 until 1945) who did thousands of psychic readings in which he was able to communicate with beings from the other side.

3. Clairsentience: this is the ability to feel vibrations of others, on an empathic level. This can involve picking up on the sensations of others on a physical or emotional level.

What are signs we are being communicated with?

During the mourning process, it's really hard to acknowledge that our parent is really gone. To imagine a world without our beloved father in it and to be able to see beyond that reality, is extremely difficult while we are experiencing intense grief. However, once the shock, grief and disbelief subsides, this is where it gets interesting. This is when one starts contemplating the existence of life after death, including concepts of immortality and eternity as we can comprehend it. While we start musing these questions, it's a good idea to get together with who can identify with our experiences.

What I discovered when I had the guts to start mentioning things of a spiritual existential nature, was that others had similar interesting experiences in receiving messages and signs from beyond. Here's the issue, that once you have to have moved through the grief to be open to these messages, seemingly strange co-incidental events will start to happen. There will be events, signs and instances of communications that you can't explain. This is the sign that you are being communicated with. Once this happens, and you discuss this with others, they will start opening up about the strange events going on around them as well. We can be communicated with in many ways, and this communication can come in the form of music (co-incidental songs with special meaning playing on the radio), temperature changes, feelings of being touched, including a sensation of warmth, tingling, smells and many other signs. When these communications happen, it's important to pay attention to the meaning, and not dismiss them as some type of co-incidence.

As I never got to see my father's body, I had to turn to the belief he had not gone, and was still around me. After all, I had had no real proof that he had passed on. The more I started to rely on spiritual signs, the more I stopped believing that his existence ended in that coffin. For those of you dubious about the spiritual part of life, perhaps this is the time to sit back, quiet yourself, and see what happens next, as you expectantly wait for a sign from your deceased parent from the other side. If you are expectant about it, that sign will come. It's only a matter of time when.

Songs In Our Head

One of the many ways that we are communicated with by souls on the other side, can be through thoughts suddenly appearing in our heads out of nowhere. Here were some of the signs I had. About three months after my father passed away, I was getting ready to go to work and was applying makeup in the bathroom when I very clearly heard, in my father's voice "What's new, pussycat?". Yes, as embarrassed as I am to admit that was my father's pet name for me, when I was very young (based off the Tom Jones song from the early sixties), I was also extremely happy to have received the message from him. I had not thought of that song or the nickname he had for me in decades. I did not hear the song on the radio, and it was quite clearly in my father's voice. There was no way for me to dispute the message, as it was in his voice, a much younger voice which sounded chirpy and upbeat. Another time, in the middle of the night, I woke up to a very loud rendering of the Bee Gee's "I gotta get a message to you". It was very strange, and was completely out of place. This is another way I believe that my father was trying to reach me.

Finding Incidental Items with Significant Meaning

A month later, once again getting ready to go to work, another definite sign of communication occurred. My husband had decided to walk our dogs, and on the walk, something caught the dogs attention. He stopped and looked down at what they were sniffing, and there was a dog collar with a tag that had obviously slipped off a dog from the neighborhood. He handed the tag to me saying "I think you might want to give this number a call". The name on the tab was Digby, which happened to be the last dog my parents had. They had named their dog Digby, which is such an unusual name back in South Africa, and even more unusual here in the USA. In fact, my husband had never even heard the name before, and here it was belonging to a dog in the neighborhood. It could have been any dog name such as Fido, Marley, Jake, Rocky, and the list goes on. What are the odds that such an unusual dog name which had very significant meaning to me, would end up in my hands? Very slim odds. Another direct message from my father. There are no coincidences!

I ended up speaking with a medium who told me my father would guide me by showing me dimes. Not pennies, but dimes. That night, walking down a dark street, I looked down and saw something glinting on the ground. You've guessed it, a dime. From that time on, I have lost track of how many dimes have shown up in completely unusual places. I have said prayers asking to hear from my father and within 60 seconds, found a dime in front of me. Walking down the elevator at a mall, feeling particularly sad that day, I heard something drop, looked down, and there was a dime. There's no doubt in my mind that we are constantly being communicated with our loved ones and guides from the other side. Even my husband, the skeptic, found dimes falling out of his car door as he was getting into his car.

Communication with Pets

Here is a quite unusual incident mentioned from a friend. Her father loved to play with her little dog. He had a specific toy he would pick up, throw and the little dog would fetch and return the toy by dropping it in front of him. After her father's passing, the dog would pick up the toy, drop it at the base of her father's favorite chair, and stare expectantly up at the chair, as if her father was sitting there waiting for him to pick up the toy and throw it. The dog was seeing something that no-one else could. She observed several other events happening in her household, all indicating her father's presence being there.

Communication by smell

Many times, contact from the other side can be in the form of smell. For instance, the smell of a certain food that a beloved family member used to make, or the smell of something that sharply brings up the memories of the past. In my case, I used to smell my grandmother's kitchen from time to time, and I immediately knew she had paid me a visit. These smells can suddenly appear and seem completely out of place from what is in the immediate environment around one.

If no more contact is made, and years go by, it could be likely that the spirit of the loved one has re-incarnated again.
When there is a very strong bond of love, if you are open to it, you will see signs of communication from your loved one, especially a parent you were close to. Imagine what chaos it would be if the dead were freely allowed to communicate with everyone? So only a special few have the gift of medium ship. The rest of us, are probably better off without it. Look carefully for signs. Be observant and aware, and it won't be long before you start noticing unusual things happening around you.

All these occurrences happen far more frequently than people actually let on. The subject of communicating with the deceased is a taboo one, although it is becoming more commonplace today, with the instant access of shared information worldwide. Many who have lost a parent have had strange experiences that cannot be explained. These signs from beyond can bring a sense of relief that the parent has gone somewhere tangible and is happy and okay.

In conclusion, there are many signs being sent by deceased loved ones all the time. Just because the curtain between life and death remains closed, messages and signs can get through. These signs bring re-assurance and comfort to us, and should be welcomed and not feared. If you look for the signs, you will find them.

11 THE HIDDEN SPIRITUAL SIDE

You are not a human on a spiritual journey
You are a spirit on a human journey..

Unknown

Ten years ago, when I went to a psychic for a reading, I got much
more than I ever bargained for. When I walked out of there, the
sky was a different color, the world a different place, and my life
was changed forever.

The above incident happened to me when I went to see a psychic
here in Los Angeles about ten years ago. Gary Spivey (I promised
to mention him, so here it is) was a very well known psychic
living in the Los Angeles area at the time, and the experience was
unlike anything I had ever imagined. The concept of any type of
existence after death had been completely hidden from me, that is
until that day. I asked him about a friend of mine who had passed,
and after he told me a couple of completely correct things, such
as how he died, what he died of, it was only then that the life
changing, belief changing event happened. I felt a rush of air go
through me, only it wasn't air. It felt like I was a human sieve,
and something drained completely through me. It was almost like
walking into a wind that wasn't cold. I sat there in shock, and at
that moment, Gary casually said to me (he was sitting across
quite a large room, about 15 feet away) "Oh, did you feel that?". I
answered in shock "Yes, what was that??!!!". He said "That was
just your friend saying hi." The rest of the discussion was a vague

blur to me. We finished up the session, and I walked outside and looked up at the sky. In that moment, it was like curtain to the other side had opened and let me see in. I was in complete shock for days afterwards, then got over it as it became a memory to me. My perception of life had changed because I had only considered the world as what I saw in front of me. Now I had to contemplate and absorb the fact that there's an entire world I couldn't see, but that did indeed exist.

Near Death Experiences (NDE's)

Many reported near death experiences have very similar settings. People are in some type of accident or bad state of health and actually die according to the medical definition of death. Their heart stops, and they are clinically pronounced dead. They report floating above their bodies, looking down on hospital staff trying to revive them, and can accurately remember conversations that took place during the chaotic revival attempts. There is a feeling of being pulled into and through a tunnel, where loved ones wait for them. Being told by heavenly beings, that this is not their time, they return back to their bodies and awaken, much to the surprise of those around them.

Many do not want to talk about these experiences, for the fear of being ridiculed and made fun of. There are wonderful varied descriptions of heaven and stories of the mansions therein. It's described as an amazing beautiful experience which leaves one with hope and comfort about the prospect of dying. From these experiences, people report coming back with psychic abilities and visions of the future. Based on modern medical technological abilities to revive people, more and more cases of NDE's are being reported than ever before.

Re-incarnation as a natural process of life

When we're very young, there is still a sense of spirituality left in us from the many previous lives that we have lived. There have been thousands of documented reports of children recalling past lives, as well as the times in-between lives.

Fifty years ago it was completely taboo to discuss the topic of reincarnation or even write about it. In today's times, these topic have become normal, although people still proceed with trepidation in mentioning it in company for the first time. It was seemingly heretical to believe in reincarnation, even though millions of people in the eastern cultures have always believed in having past lives. The Dalai Lama maintains in the Tibetan Book of Living and Dying, that death is a normal process that will occur as long as you are a human being, and that it is pointless to worry about it, as it is inevitable. Re-incarnation is like changing your clothes at the end of the day, or walking from one movie into another, with your life playing on the screen.

We are so scared of what happens to us when we die, that this fear keeps us from truly living. If we can truly understand the significance of re-incarnation in our lives, then we can understand that we continue to exist, after our deaths. It's not over when we die. There is a part of us that does not die with the body, even though it feels like that to us while we are still living. The physical body suit we live in starts decaying from the time we are born. It's merely a shell, in which our soul can peer out through our eyes into the physical world. When we are born, most of us have loving eyes and smiling faces welcoming us. When we die, we have the loving eyes and smiling faces welcoming us back to the other side. We are never alone.

Dr Brian Weiss, the author of Many Lives, Many Masters, discovered past lives in his patients by regressing them through hypnosis. He was amazed when going through the past life experiences of the individual people he regressed that ailments started disappearing.

Ramifications of Reincarnation

As we age, and approach death and the unknown, we know that an inevitable demise is facing us. We fear that final moment and the last breath we take as a human. I honestly believe that once we understand the ramifications of re-incarnation, that there is a feeling of excitement about what the choices of our next lifetime could be. There is also a feeling of really wanting to live this life well, so karmic lessons will be completed. We all have a life plan when we arrive, we just have to figure out what it is, and make our choices accordingly.

The concept of our existences over many lifetimes, is to learn the necessary lessons, and rise up through the spiritual ranks until we are once more re-united with our creator. The only way through these ranks is to have unconditional love and forgiveness to our fellow beings. We learn these emotions through the relationships we have. It's not easy to forgive someone who you feel has truly hurt you, but unless it can be done one can never truly progress onto the next spiritual level. When life dishes out hardships to us, we get to learn from those events. A closed door opens a door to a new opportunity which will ultimately lead us in a new direction. A death of a loved one might inspire us to move in the direction of our life's mission. We are not meant to just suffer and be miserable, we are also meant to experience love and joy in this lifetime.

Our bodies are merely shells, in which we exist to experience love. We are not our bodies, but are spiritual beings encased in a physical presence on a temporary basis. There is a beginning to the process of our bodies, and an end. If you take the time to be still and observe the world around you through the eyes of your body, you will really understand the impermanence of your physical existence, and the permanence of your non-physical one.

Losses are lessons

Many times we wonder why we have to experience agonizing grief, sorrow and losses. We wonder why some die young, and others die violently. Who are the lessons for? The answer is that these are lessons for the ones left behind. These life lessons teach us how to experience certain situations that may not have been experienced in different lifetimes. When a good friend of ours dies young, it could be a lesson for us to be able to deal with the trauma of that loss. A similar thing could apply to a parent who loses a baby that only lived a couple of months, or a child that dies a violent death. There is always a lesson in every experience.

The Law of Karma

As I was growing up, my parents taught me about the Law of Karma. Their interpretation of Karma was that if someone treated you badly, you just had to sit back and wait until Karma got them. Many times, something bad would had happen to an individual, and they would say "There, you see, that's Karma!" As a society we use the word instant Karma which we perceive as instant retribution for a wrong. In the re-incarnation principle of Karma, karmic events happen across lifetimes. Your thoughts and actions in previous lives can very well determine what happens to you in the next lifetime.

If we truly understood this wouldn't we treat others with more tolerance and understanding? Wouldn't we be kinder to those who have very little for fear that in our next lifetime that may be us? Wouldn't we give more to others in need, knowing that it will always come back to us? Every action we take during our lifetimes, will bring an equal reaction, whether it be good or bad. As the bible verse goes "What you reap, so shall you sow", the energy we put forth will have a direct result in response. This is where the original law which states "Treat others as you wish to be treated" comes from. The law of Karma is one of the spiritual laws of life.

You can't advance spiritually while you're angry at someone Go with the flow. When you stop resisting and go with the flow everything in your life will fall in place

The Master Plan

When we first incarnate as physical beings, it's done according to our life master plan. Our lives are designed to be part of a master plan. All the major life events that are meant to happen are planned. The smaller events are free will. This master plan consists of arrangements we have made with other soul mates before we are reincarnated into the next lifetime. As covered before, when good things happen we tend to think of those events as serendipitous or happenstance. How about if we thought of those instances as some sort of divine decree, an event long planned?

In Greek mythology, the River of Forgetfulness is discussed as what people drank from to forget their previous life, in order to start their next life with oblivion to the many previous lives experienced. During the time after crossing over from physical to non-physical, there is great planning to make up for lessons not learned in the previous lifetime. These plans made with the soul mates that are meant to reincarnate together in the upcoming lifetime.

Specifics of the Master Plan

The Master plan consists of a timeline of major life events that are to occur during the upcoming lifetime. There may be losses, joys, loves, distresses, difficult choices to be made and strengthening challenges to be faced. The major events of life are learning experiences, which are important to move the individual along the pre-planned journey. Your actions in-between those major life events, including your relationships to other people, how you conduct yourself, what you say and how you treat others is up to you. There has to be free will in order for you to learn from the benefits of mistakes. Every life is a learning process, and is a necessity in order for us to advance spiritually.

The people in our lives that particularly exasperate us, such as a boss, co-worker, our parents, family and friends are all carefully picked by us. We plan carefully as to how the main events happen, and how a particular soul mate is to come into our life. It may happen early in our lives, within our immediate families, or it may happen later in our life when we somehow "by coincidence" meet someone who is to have a large impact on our lives.

We may wonder why a particularly painful event would happen to us, seemingly out of the blue. For instance, we lost a baby, or a sibling, or parent at a young age. All of those events happen for a very specific reason, and one has to look at what the lesson to be learned is (or was). Perhaps someone is born with a disability, or has been maimed in an accident. This could be as a result of being intolerant to people with disabilities in a previous life, or could be in order to teach another tolerance. In these cases one might argue that the accident happened as a result of free will. The Master Plan consists of the major events that happen to us, which seem out of our control. The more minor events, such as how we react to our daily lives, are up to free will.

Spiritual phenomenon have always existed

Talking about spirits and spiritual things is not something new. Since the beginning of time, man has pondered to much extent about the world that is hidden from us.

The following excerpts were written by a man called Léon-Dénizarth-Hippolyte with his nom de plume of Allan Kardec. He lived in Lyons from 1804 to 1869. His friend had two daughters who had become mediums and were transmitting information that was specifically for him. He drew up a series of questions to ask these spirits and here are a few of them from "The Mediums Book", in the numerical sequences that they appear in the actual writings.

It is a mistake to suppose that a man must be a medium in order to attract to himself the beings of the invisible world. Space is peopled with spirits; they are always around us, always beside us; they see us and watch us; they mingle in our meetings, and follow or avoid us, according as we attract or repel them.

1. Can spirits be evoked by those who are not mediums?
"Every one can evoke spirits; and if those whom you call cannot manifest themselves physically, they are none the less near you, and hear your call."

15. Can spirits tell us of our past existences?
"God sometimes, for a special object, permits those existences to be revealed to you. When such knowledge will conduce to your instruction and edification, the revelation is permitted; but, in

such cases, it always comes to you spontaneously, and in some unforeseen manner. It is never permitted for the satisfaction of mere curiosity."

He drew up a series of similar questions to ask these channeled spirits from a book called "The Spirits Book".

2. What is to be understood by infinity?
"That which has neither beginning nor end; the unknown: all that is unknown is infinite."

18. Will man ever be able to penetrate the mystery of things now hidden from him?
"The veil will be raised for him in proportion as he accomplishes his purification; but, in order to understand certain things, he would need faculties which he does not yet possess."

78. Have spirits had a beginning, or have they existed, like God, from all eternity?
"If spirits had not had a beginning, they would be equal with God; whereas they are His creation, and subject to His will. That God has existed from all eternity is incontestable; but as to when and how He created us, we know nothing. You may say that we have had no beginning in this sense, that, God being eternal, He must have incessantly created. But as to when and how each of us was made, this, I repeat, is known to no one. It is the great mystery."

80. Is the creation of spirits always going on, or did it only take place at the beginning of time?
"It is always going on, that is to say, God has never ceased to create."

87. Do spirits occupy a determinate and circumscribed region in space?

"Spirits are everywhere; the infinitudes of space are peopled with them in infinite numbers. Unperceived by you, they are incessantly beside you, observing and acting upon you; for spirits are one of the powers of Nature, and are the instruments employed by God for the accomplishment of His providential designs.

What I find fascinating about these writings is that they were done over 150 years ago. Read the entire works written by Allan Kardec at http://www.spiritwritings.com/kardec.html

In all of recorded time, not a lot has really changed, except the name of the phenomenon, which now is popularly categorized as "Metaphysics". In the early two thousands "The Law of Attraction" became trendy (although it has always existed), whereby like attracts like, and your thinking manifests items and events into reality based on the focus of your thoughts. The metaphysical categories of books are now filled with endless writings of musings about what happens after death, spirits, medium ship, law of attraction, and quantum physics. There are books written about past lives, future lives, lives in between incarnations, near death experiences and many other mystical topics.

 Nothing really has changed in all the centuries, other than our consciousness is evolving, and more people are tuning in to the possibilities of knowing things that were forbidden to be contemplated or even be mentioned in earlier times. The metaphysical writings of past times were considered heretical to the church even though mention was made of such things in the new testament. Many people were burnt at the stake for being witches for considering such things.

According to polls, over 80% of Americans believe in life after death, and around 25% of Americans believe in reincarnation. I believe a lot of this is due to a new awareness that has connected us through the internet, and the easily available information now at our fingertips.

Finding our spiritual path

Up until most recently in the western world, finding one's spiritual path was reserved only for those who were lost. Today, it's become fashionable and trendy. Celebrities walk around with Kabbalah bracelets, while books like "The Secret" with the law of attraction become best sellers. If you look on Amazon under the category "New Age", 56,000 or so books appear. Under the category of spirituality, over 140,000 books are listed. It's no longer difficult or unobtainable to find topics that would have been forbidden and taboo a mere hundred years ago.

We as human beings, are trying to reach a higher level of consciousness now more than ever before. We are all trying to make sense of the chaos and confusion of the world destruction around us, and the point of our own existence. Perhaps one day, this higher sense of consciousness will serve to re-unite mankind, and bring greater awareness to the concepts of that what we do to hurt one, hurts all. We can only hope so. We have enough resources to feed the world, and yet we hold onto those resources believing we won't have enough for ourselves. We fight and kill our fellow man to take over their countries and establish dominance over them. How different would the world be if we realized when we kill others that we kill part of ourselves, because our spirits all come from the same source. We are all part of the same creation, but because we are different physically from each other, we condemn one another. The next time you look at someone, really see them. See their hopes, joys, fears, longing, happiness and all the other emotions that exude from that person, and you will notice how in the end, we all want the same thing, happiness and love. If we could truly realize how interconnected we are, we would not only change the way we perceive others, but also ourselves.

Forgiveness is Spiritual Nirvana

In our lifetimes as adults, we build up so many resentments towards others. We carry that anger like a heavy rock in our hearts. It's important to let go of the anger or revenge, wanting to somehow get even with those who we perceive as having harmed us. Learning how to forgive is really the best anyone can do with their spiritual lives. When you forgive someone, you get to move on with your own life without looking back. You have cleaned your side of the street and can now focus on other issues standing between you and your happiness.

Sometimes it's very hard to acknowledge when one is wrong, or sometimes one is wrong and it's hard to acknowledge that too. When someone has hurt us, or injured us on a very deep level, we carry that as a heavy betrayal and burden and we feel a sense of great unfairness in the situation. Whatever the situation is, know that the solution is always the same. Letting go of these ill feelings towards others can be very difficult. Lack of forgiveness can destroy wellbeing, family bonds, friendships and so many other relationships. Know that answer is always forgiveness.

Forgiveness changes our Karmic Cycle, and helps us to live peaceful lives. It returns our squandered energy to us, which was previously wasted on futile anger, harbored resentments and thoughts of getting even. Learning to forgive transgressions against us reminds us that we can't change other people's behavior and that we need to accept them the way they are. Forgiveness also helps us to forget the painful events of our pasts and pave the way towards a healthy and happy future away from misery. It is totally your choice whether you choose to forgive others, but if you do, you move yourself that much closer to a life filled with purpose, a life of joy and most importantly of all, a life of meaning. Regard forgiveness as a selfish act of spiritual pleasure, because the one who will truly benefit is you. Forgiveness truly gets you closer to spiritual nirvana as you continue to practice it on a day to day basis in your life.

"When you forgive, you in no way change the past - but you sure do change the future." -Bernard Meltzer

12 THE CASE FOR GOD

God, despite his casual silence, still exists. Of that I haven't a single doubt.

Don Williams, Jr

One day, about ten years ago, I was sitting listening to the radio in the car having just arrived at home. A song by Joan Osborne "What if God was one of us" was playing. As I was contemplating the words of the song, one of the most monumental events of my life happened. Suddenly I was transported into a very light place. It was as if the curtain to heaven had opened, and there I was, in front of the Creator, with a enormous majestic audience watching, all looking at me. Next to the Creator (God),on the right hand was the being I recognized as Jesus. I would like to emphasize, at the time of this happening, I was not a believer. It was just a story I had read in the bible in my youth, having attended a Christian school, although I was Jewish. I was unable to see the face of God, but I was aware of Him, Jesus and the whole majestic audience of millions of people were watching just me. In that moment I felt immense shame for the way I had lived my life up to now. In my consciousness, I was made aware of my longing for capitalistic material things and how unimportant these wants were in the big scheme of things. Desires for wealth and possessions all meant nothing in this realm. As I hung my head in an overwhelming immense moment of shame, my life was reviewed in front of me.
I wanted to be swallowed up by the ground, and to disappear. The gazes on me were like that of a family I had left, who were

reviewing what I had been doing in my absence. It was as if I was returning to a large heavenly family, and they were disappointed in me, although, not nearly as disappointed as I was in myself. Suddenly, I found myself sitting back in my car listening to the radio. The whole event, which had seemed like it had taken quite a while, was merely a few seconds, but had given me a view into the hereafter. It was almost like a warning to me, to change my focus to the important issues in life, as one day I would be judged. This is as close to a near death experience that I have ever had. I knew that my life needed to change, to have meaning and importance.

When we think about God we think about infinity, about all there ever was, is and will be. We wonder about where God came from, and did He just create earth or are there many other earth like planets, where there are other human being exist. We wonder why He seems so far away from us, and if he really can hear our prayers. Some of us wonder if he does exist at all, and believe in the randomness of the universe, such as the Big Bang Theory, and how are bodies and souls were merely created from a cell. Others believe we evolved from animals, being that prehistoric man was merely the next step from an Ape. Many of the answers to these questions we know, but can't acknowledge or understand. These answers are inside us, far buried from our conscious thought.

The destruction of many Bible books by Constantine

Constantine was the first Roman Emperor to convert to Christianity. He lived from 272 to 337 and began the formation of Catholicism, and the crusade to remove any book from the bible that was unacceptable. It was estimated that there were around six hundred books of which all were destroyed except for eighty. The protestant church got rid of more, bringing the final number to 66 of which the King James Bible consists of.

The Catholic church labeled these lost books as heretical and dangerous. So all that valuable part of history was destroyed, and all that is left, is what the church wanted us to know. This also conveniently fitted into the nice little package which has so many holes in it today. What was it the church did not want us to know? I'm pretty sure that the philosophies we are discovering through new age doctrines today were known about, all those centuries ago. Who was Constantine to decide what the rest of the world should or should not be allowed to know? The valuable information lost could have made a huge difference to mankind. Instead of wars over religion, we might have found peace. Instead of hate because of skin color, we might have learned to love the inner being of others. Instead of looking merely at the differences between us, we might have celebrated the similarities of our existence. People who blindly follow religion as a path, should question what was left out of the very important and significant information that was passed down. The world deserved to know what was in all of those books of the bible, and not just the ones that seemed more "appropriate".

What happened in the early years of the life of Jesus

At the time of Christ, there is little or almost no reference to his life before the meeting of John the Baptist. Why would this very important knowledge be withheld from the world, and not documented? The only reason being is that it contained knowledge which would be completely contradictory to what the church would have us believe. These contradictions could well include the fact that he worked, had a family, and lived as a regular human being. There are so many holes in the bible, and analyzing the absence of information can give us a good idea that the concepts and ideas behind the gaps, were so frightening and terrifying to the church, that it was kept absolutely secret or destroyed. Many regard the bible as an absolute work and try to make everything fit within their personal beliefs.

As we grew more sophisticated and different branches of Christianity appeared, these sects started fighting against each other and millions of lives have been lost all in the name of religion.

The reason for our creation

I heard an excerpt from a Christian radio station, where the host proclaimed everyone was born sinful, and is basically damned. These are the kind of statements that have been advocated by the church to install fear and absolute obedience, without question. If we were born imperfect, that would imply God is imperfect in that He makes imperfect things. This havoc and destruction among the human race is not what our creator wanted. War, destruction and global domination was not the reason for our existence. We exist because we wanted to and chose to have a physical experience. We chose to leave our very happy spiritual environment to experience a physical existence. Look what we have done to each other and our planet's resources. When does the destruction end? When do we implement the love and forgiveness amongst each other that helps us all grow on a spiritual level. You can't advance spiritually while you're angry at someone. Go with the flow. When you stop resisting and go with the flow everything in your life will fall in place

What the Kabbalah teaches

Many teachings including the Kabbalah (Jewish mysticism), state that we were all part of the creator (God), and once we separated from God our purpose of re-incarnating is to progress through the different spiritual levels until we are once more returned to be one with God. Kabbalah, (according to Wikipedia), is a set of esoteric teachings meant to explain the relationship between an eternal and mysterious Creator and the mortal and finite universe which He created. The teachings of Kabbalah promote re-incarnation and the migration of the soul until it reaches the highest spiritual level, which is one of reuniting with our creator.

Reincarnation in biblical times

Many biblical figures are reported to be re-incarnations of other biblical figures. For example, Esther was the re-incarnation of Eve, John the Baptist was the re-incarnation of Elijah. In fact, in Matthew 11: 13-14, Jesus states: ***"For all the Prophets and the Law prophesied until John. And if you are willing to accept it, <u>he is the Elijah who was to come</u>. He who has ears, let him hear."***

New American Standard Bible (NASB). However, John the Baptist, when directly asked if he was Elijah denied being so. So there again you have two direct contradictions in the bible. However, if the church follows everything Jesus said, then the reference to re-incarnation is literal. The church, that evolved after the death of Christ, adhered to just one teaching. People today seem to ignore the fact that certain parts of the bible were removed so as the keep the teachings absolutely literal and to keep a fierce grip on people's faith by instilling fear of damnation and hell.

Jesus did indeed teach re-incarnation, although very subtly. Many things that were said by Him, through teachings and parables, were taken very literally, and not figuratively as they were intended. When Jesus said "I and my Father are one", He was talking about God (the holy spirit) existing within him, as He does within all of us. The holy spirit which resides within us, is our original source energy, being part of God, from where we originated.

A Course of Miracles, written by Helen Schucman, talks about God being non-dualistic. The concept of forgiveness is regarded as being the way to end the continual reincarnation process and to obtain unity once more with God.

This concept of duality, which refers to the concepts of opposites, is very important. Examples are, if there is good there must be evil. If there is God, there must be Satan. If there is heaven, there must be hell, etc. Now in the bible God wants us to lead good lives in order to be one day re-united with Him. If we don't lead these lives according to what is laid out in the bible, He will be angry with us, and cast us out. So, we are created as damaged, and yet God only creates perfect things. If God stated in the old testament the foods you may not eat, yet in the new testament Jesus stated that it did not matter. How would God "change" his mind? To imply that would be to imply that God is not perfection and made a mistake. There are so many holes in religion. that in the end, all we can rely on is our inner true feelings and faith.

Reuniting the soul with our Creator

In Jeffrey Furst's book of Edgar Cayce's story of Jesus, he discusses living the law of grace, loving each other as He has loved us, or we remain under the law of Karma and keep re-incarnating, until we reach the highest spiritual level to be re-united our creator.

In Gary Renard's book Disappearance of the Universe, he discusses the concept of the world around us being completely created by our ego, as well as the separation of ourselves from our creator, where the only way to be re-united is to achieve the ultimate level of complete love and forgiveness. While I am not in complete alignment with the idea of my world being completely fabricated, I am in alignment of our world being manipulated by our consciousness.

There are times when I feel myself feeling almost disembodied, and realize how temporary our lives are. If you can focus on the moment reflecting and meditating, you can almost feel a sense of being looking out through your eyes at the outside world around you as if you were a temporary resident inside your body. This would be almost as if you are a visitor looking out at the world through the eyes of temporary shell you have inhabited, travelling around your lifetime all on a temporary basis. How much kinder would we be to others, knowing that the essence of ourselves is all part of the same originating entity, and the bodies we assume, are merely temporary pieces of clothing which we discard in the matter of seven or eight decades. If we truly understood how temporary our lives are, would we bother with wars, grudges, anger and revenge against our fellow man? Would we care about the color of our skin, whether we were rich or poor, famous or unknown?

None of this is what God wanted for us. He wanted us to love each other, and live in peace. None of which is happening in the world today.

Where God is today

God is still around. He hasn't left, and still watches over us. So many people in history have dual interpretations of God, as being an angry God, a jealous God, as well as a loving God. A good loving God would not do anything harmful to us, like punishing us and sending us to hell. A loving God would not allow children to be born, only to be sent to hell because they were not baptized, or had never heard of Jesus. A loving God would not want us to kill our fellow man in His name. Death, sorrow and misery, would not be intentionally bestowed on us by God. All the things we as human beings experience are because of our own desires manifested. We desired to leave heaven and come to earth, and so we did. We manifested our physical creation into human form. Our hell is here on earth, and our heaven is when we leave hell (earth)and return to our heavenly family and our Creator.

We are all given little glimpses of heaven and God in our lifetime, maybe the smile of a baby, a beautiful sunrise, a friendly face in a group of strangers. There are no real answers to the mystery of life other than that we are in it for a short period of time, and then we are gone. God not only exists in heaven, but also inside each one of us. We contain the Holy Spirit inside of us, as we are all part of God. It was our choice to leave God, and He waits for us to return, no matter by which path we choose.

What God wants from us

Many times throughout life, our existence is questioned. We wonder what our life purpose is, and why we were created. If God is looking down on us, with all the wars, anger and hate occurring on the planet right now, how could we be doing anything pleasing in His eyes. So what does God want from us other than to return to him? He wants us to obey his commandments and live in a spirit of love and forgiveness with one another. Forgiveness is the greatest human emotion that we could possibly experience. With forgiveness we can truly get closer to God. We are constantly in need of renewing our faith in an almighty creator. When events happen in our lives that we just do not understand, our faith is tested.

Wherever we are today in our lives, is a destination as to where our actions and thoughts have brought us. If we truly believe in the non-physical majesty of heaven, why not believe in the physical majesty of earth? God definitely wants us to be happy, and enjoy the life we have. The suffering we experience as a result of our Karma is from our doing, not God's. Sometimes when we are really quiet, the answers to the questions of life can be heard within because we all carry the history of the world, as well as the presence of God within us. Our decisions and choices in life are our own, and free will determines our path between the major events of our life, as mentioned previously within the "Master Plan" section.

Forgiving as we have been Forgiven

Forgiving others who have hurt us could be the single most important lesson to learn in life. Until we learn how to forgive, we are stuck in a cycle of anger and retribution for past events. True forgiveness of others and towards ourselves, is the closest we can ever get to being one with God. God wants us to be able to love one another because without love, life becomes meaningless.

We've taken God out of everything. Our schools are Godless, and children are devoid of spiritual growth, and the incidents of violent crimes in the nation have increased. There are shootings in schools and colleges that have no justification whatsoever. It seems that when prayer stops, everything spirals out of control. If we could teach the next generation the value of introspection, perhaps they would be the ones to change the destructive path towards which our world is hurtling. Perhaps the time has come to reconsider incorporating religion and spiritual values in the next generations.

13 THE LIST

Let go of the past and go for the future. Go confidently in the direction of your dreams. Live the life you imagined.

Henry David Thoreau

One of the best things I did for myself was to make "The List", which was a summary of all the things I want to do before I am unable to. Everyone should have a list, a reason for living, loving and partaking in life's amazing journey.

Many people feel the need to set goals. Goal setting has been embraced much by the business world as well as those who are achievement orientated. Goal setting can be for personal development, as a tool to help one achieve your dreams. Many motivational gurus such as Brian Tracy state to write down 125 goals fold up the paper, and revisit them in a year, to see what has been achieved in that time frame. Then there's the argument about whether the goals should be realistic, or whether you should reach for the stars. Both of these mindsets have advantages and disadvantages to be considered.

While I agree, it's good to set yearly goals as well as monthly, weekly and daily goals, it's also good to set life goals. Goal setting is a powerful process toward identifying your future. There are many articles and books on how to do this for business and personal objectives in order to achieve great successes. The purpose of goal setting is to help direct you specifically to your desired results.

Yes, goal setting can give you a sense of purpose and help you cultivate meaning, but this is not what "The List" is about. This is not "The Bucket List", which was the movie with actors Jack Nicholson and Morgan Freeman, who created a list of things to do before they "Kicked the Bucket". This is about creating a list of things to do to make your life complete, worthwhile, and worth remembering. This is not about something you leave until your life is almost over, so that you have regrets about what you have not done or accomplished. "The List" is about what you have to do to actively make the most of the life you have right now.

You were born for a reason. You manifested into this body not just to be an observer looking out at the world, but also to be a participant. The human shell that you wear as clothing is there for a specific reason, to enable you to physically partake in the activities of the world. There is a reason you are alive. If you were born to just exist, to sit in front of the television, eat, work and sleep, then what would be the point of your life, your existence and being? One of the positive things about experiencing the loss of a parent, is that it is inspirational to help change and define ones life's purpose. Having a purpose to living is what makes us look forward to the future with excitement and anticipation. Your parent's death can be a catalyst to inspire huge life changes, including ones you were to afraid to do, such as changing careers, or leaving unhealthy relationships.

I asked my father three months before he passed, if he could go back 30 years in time, what he would do. His face lit up at the thought of having 30 more years to do whatever he wanted to do, and he gave me his answer. Don't let that be you at the end of your life, answering with what could only be a impossible dream. Make it a reality, something which can happen now and in the immediate future of your life.

Page | 145

How to come up with The List

How do you get started? Easy, you daydream. You think about all the things in your life that you would like to do. Contemplate what makes you excited, what makes you want to lean forward and join a conversation. Think about TV shows of places you would like to see, movies about adventures you'd like to have, books about interesting subjects you would like to explore. So many times in your life, someone has mentioned something that has resonated with you. You then take that thought and discard it into the "not possible" section of your brain. Go to the "not possible" part of your brain and withdraw all the thoughts you have tossed into there during your lifetime. Retrieve them and then write them down. It has to be in the form of a list, with the most desired items near the top.

The Specifics of The List

You don't have to advance through the list sequentially, but at your own pace. "The List" is going to become an important part of your life. It's not something you are going to leave in a drawer somewhere. You need to have your list in open sight, where you can reference it often. The idea behind the list is to make you excited about living. You've been through the grief, and mourning of someone who no longer has the opportunity of dreaming. This is your time to take hold of your dreams, hopes and fantasies and make them real, so that one day when you die, people will remember how much you lived.

There is no need to base your list on someone else's goals. This list is unique to you and what you want, not what someone else wants. Pay attention to your gut feelings about people, places and things, and use those gut feelings to help you establish your list.

The List is going to move you out of your comfort zone and into the exciting world of the unknown, your unknown. If you need to visualize your list, then do so with pictures, goal boards, and any other strategies that will start the creative process within you.

This is not about manifestations, although I do believe that works, but is more about you deciding what you want to take action on, and moving forward from there. Hoping and wishing from your sofa just won't be enough. The vision starts in your mind. You think the thought then you write it down. You need to make the list of these thoughts and let yourself be motivated constantly by it. You'll be amazed at what you can achieve merely by deciding you want to do so. Your list needs to encompass your passions in life. Not all the items on your list will revolve around having money to do certain things. Some items will need time, patience, motivation and enthusiasm, rather than money.

Write the list in the following way

The items on your list should be written not as wishes, or wants, but as events, such as the following:

- Write the items on the list in the present tense, as if the goal is happening at this moment.
- Be as detailed as you want. The more energy and detail you put into each item, the more sure you will be of whether that is something you really want to achieve.
- Be realistic or unrealistic. It's your list. It's your mind. It's your ideas.
- Once you start writing other ideas will come to mind. Put those down too. You get to sort your list into your order of preference and priority.

Here's my List

To give you an example of the list, I have written down some of my own. My list changes often. I might see something in a movie, or in a magazine, and go "Oh wow! I would love to do that!" This starts the idea which then becomes more and more detailed in my mind. That's the whole idea, to live your life and notice things around you that give you joy. Here is my current list. Some of the items have already been achieved.

1. Sit overlooking the Tuscany valley in Italy, watching the sunset, with a glass of cabernet sauvignon in my hand.
2. Touch the great wailing wall in Israel.
3. See the Mona Lisa in the Louvre in Paris.
4. Sit at a sidewalk cafe in Paris eating French baguettes, drinking wine and watching the people walk by.
5. See the pyramids in Egypt.
6. See Mount Rushmore.
7. Spend two weeks on a tropical island writing a novel.
8. Spend two weeks on a mission in Central Africa helping underprivileged people.
9. See the Redwood forest in Northern California
10. Go to a Broadway play in New York.
11. Write an inspiring book that will uplift others.
12. Write a screenplay that is turned into movie.
13. Have a meeting with the Dalai Lama.
14. Attend Christmas midnight mass at the Vatican.
15. Take a RV to Area 51, park on top of a hill and watch for UFO's.
16. Watch the balloons rise at the International Balloon Fiesta in Albuquerque, New Mexico
17. See the statue of Christ The Redeemer in Rio de Janeiro
18. Volunteer with the elderly.
19. Unconditionally help others, without expectation of anything in return, by being a silent giver.

What will your list be like? When will you start? Hopefully, if anything good comes out of the immense loss you have suffered in your life, it will be the awakening of your spiritual and physical nature. Hopefully this will allow you to regard the rest of your own personal journey as an adventure for living life in the most audacious way that you can.

Will I see you in the Tuscany Valley and raise my glass to you? I hope so. I hope you live the rest of your life looking forward to the future while embracing your loss and never forgetting the parent that will live on in your heart forever, who inspired you to live. One of the things you can do in memory of the parent you have lost, is committing to live more intensely and make your life have more meaning, to honor them.

14 WHERE TO NOW

Moving on from a chapter in the past, is not closing the book but just turning the page.

Unknown

I am an old lady in my late seventies. It is a dark night, and I lie floating in a swimming pool watching a million stars glitter in the night sky. I look down at my body, which as aged, but not badly. Next to the swimming pool is a large single level family home with a lovely large area of well manicured lawn. I turn my head and look over at the home, and from the brightly lit windows I can hear the sounds of children yelling and laughing. In the background is the sound of hairdryers going as young ladies prepare for an evening out with their friends. It feels so comforting hearing those sounds. As I lie there floating on my back, with the water gently lapping around me, I wonder why I am here. The home looks familiar to me. It suddenly dawns on me that this is the home I grew up in, and the voices in that home are my own and my siblings.

I look up again into the sky and something catches my attention. I narrow my eyes trying to make out what I am seeing. In the sky I notice that one star is exceedingly brighter than the rest. Suddenly, the brightness grows larger and larger and I am watching in awe as the brilliance of the star grows. A beam of light slowly starts shining down on me. I look up in shock at the beam which is now growing larger and shining brightly on me. The beam now envelopes me and all I can see is a large area of

bright white light. I look back at the house with the sounds in the distance, and look back up into light. I'm struck with shock and a realization that it's my time. My whole life has gone by.
I say almost in a whisper "It's my time, isn't it?" There's no response. My eyes fill with tears. A few moments go by. "I'm not ready. Please ....give me some more time" My voice gets louder."I haven't achieved my life's mission yet ...please...there's so much more I could still do…" There's still no response. I feel such anguish and regret with the knowledge that I had not yet achieved what I should have, and that I was not worthy to go into that light. The tears run down my face, and once more I say weakly "Please.....give me just one more chance, just one more chance….please"

Seconds go by and I notice that nothing is happening. I wasn't being pulled into the light. Slowly, the large brightness of the beam on me is subsiding, and its size and intensity is reducing. It's fading and shrinking and in a small amount of time it's back to being the same size as all the other stars blending into the perfect summers night sky. I sit up sobbing in my bed. I look around at the morning light filtering into my bedroom window. I'm young again, and my whole life is ahead of me, and so the journey begins

The passage above came from an actual dream I had about 8 years ago. I woke up sobbing, and immediately realized the symbolism of the dream. It's about determining your life's purpose and feeling you have achieved what you were brought here to do.

After the above event, an emotional and spiritual awakening happened. I was determined to live life to the fullest as there is an end, and it could come all too quickly. I started Scuba Diving, traveling to tropical islands with people I didn't know. I bought a Harley and became a weekend warrior, and even took some long road trips. My friend and family were horrified about that adventure.

No Man Is An Island

It's true that while it's good to be independent, it's also good to have very stable grounded relationships, especially progressing through the mourning period.

We all start life in the same way, and it is the way we proceed with the journey, that makes the difference in the end. We are ever evolving as a human race, with much to learn and many new things to discover. If we look at how far mankind as evolved, and the great and wonderful things (not the destructive events) we, as human beings have achieved, we can only look forward with great expectation and hope into the future as our relationships become interconnected and evolved amidst the dawning of a new spiritual era.

If people don't understand what you have been though, and are going through, keep this in mind, that someday they will know. Losing a parent is a fate that will, without fail, happen to all of the human race. Just because someone doesn't know how to deal with the grief of another, that attitude will change with their own loss, as will their ability to empathize with other peoples experiences.

Sometimes we are so scared of dying and what happens to us after that, that we really forget to really live our life. Once we have passed through the grieving stage, then the thought of really living starts to emerge. When we consider how to really live, we start to formulate a plan as to how we will progress through the rest of our days. How we enjoy the remainder of our lives is up to us. We can choose unhappiness or misery, or we can choose joy, excitement and adventure. I don't know about you, but I choose the latter, which I'm sure would be in alignment with my father would want for me.

Being loving and compassionate to each other

If there is anything this journey has taught us, it's to be more understanding and compassionate with others. Our eyes have been opened to one of the truly greatest sorrows in life, that of losing one's father. We have now crossed over into a previously unknown realm of sorrow, which has awakened us to the concept of being kinder and having increased empathy to others, because of a new understanding we have acquired.

One of the things you can do in memory of the parent you have lost, is committing to live more intensely and make your life have more meaning, to honor them. There is an amazing life waiting for you out there. Grab it, run with it, and look forward to the future with hope.

CONCLUSION

At the time of this writing, it's been 11 months since my father passed away. Although I have made great strides through my bereavement period, there are still sad, pensive moments.

My life is a lot happier now, and I laugh and enjoy the company of friends and family. I still cry on the occasion but for the most part, life is really good. I fully understand and comprehend the fact that dying is part of living, and the losses we experience define and mold us into the people we are.

One thing I know for sure is that my father loved life with a passion. For me to spend too much of my time being sad about his physical presence no longer being around, especially as his spiritual presence is, would be a waste of very productive energy. I am fully aware that the true mourning for him will continue for a while, but the strength and insight I have gained will in the end be worth the sadness and loss experienced.

I wish you a speedy recovery through your journey of grief. Everyone, without exception will experience your pain sooner or later. Reach out to others who are going through the same experience, and you will be comforted in the realization that you are not alone. Seek out the joy of life, and make the rest of your journey here matter.

Love and light

Mandy

REFERENCE LIST

Website Information Sources

healingresources.info/emotional_trauma_overview.htm

www.cancer.gov/cancertopics/pdq/supportivecare/bereavement/Patient/page2

www.mirnabard.com/2010/04/99-favorite-social-media-quotes-and-tips/

livinginspirit.wordpress.com/

www.ilasting.com/

www.griefshare.org/

www.griefnet.org/

www.ards.org/links/griefhealing/

www.journeyofhearts.org/

www.hospicefoundation.org

www.aarp.org/relationships/grief-loss/

www.webhealing.com/

www.bereavement-poems-articles.com/

www.tampabay.com/blogs/media/content/grief-and-loss-social-media-how-facebook-and-twitter-can-help-cope-serious-loss

www.biblegateway.com/versions/New-International-Version-NIV-Bible/

Recommended Reading list

Dr Brian Weiss; Many lives, Many Masters
Judy Tatelbaum; The Courage to Grieve
Carole J. Obley; I'm still with you
Mark Anthony; Never Letting Go
Jeffrey Long,MD; Evidence of the Afterlife
Brook Noel; I Wasn't Ready to Say Goodbye
Carol Bowman; Return from Heaven
Raymond Moody, Elizabeth Kubler Ross; Life after Life
Jennifer Skiff; God Stories: Inspiring Encounters with the Divine
Esther and Jerry Hicks; The Vortex
Jane Roberts; Seth Speaks
Therese A. Rando; How To Go on Living When Someone You
Love dies

Made in the USA
San Bernardino, CA
23 December 2015